Desert Plants

of Egypt's Wadi El Gemal National Park

Desert Plants
of Egypt's Wadi El Gemal National Park

Tamer Mahmoud

The American University in Cairo Press
Cairo New York

Comments and questions can be addressed to the author at:
tamer_mahmed@yahoo.com

First published in 2010 by
The American University in Cairo Press
113 Sharia Kasr el Aini, Cairo, Egypt
420 Fifth Avenue, New York, NY 10018
www.aucpress.com

Dar el Kutub No. 14130/09
ISBN 978 977 416 350 0

Dar el Kutub Cataloging-in-Publication Data

Mahmoud, Tamer
Desert Plants of Egypt's Wadi El Gemal National Park / Tamer Mahmoud.—Cairo: The American University in Cairo Press, 2010
p. cm.
ISBN 978 977 416 350 0
1. National Parks and Reserves—Wadi El Gemal (Egypt)
581.716533

1 2 3 4 5 6 15 14 13 12 11 10

Designed by Sally Boylan
Printed in Egypt

This work is dedicated to the memory of my colleagues, all of whom died in the line of duty:

Mostafa Ramadan (1980–2002)
Ali Sallam (1970–2003)
Osman Hassay (1979–2006)
Mohammed Abdel Sattar (1971–2006)

We will never forget you.

Contents

Foreword ix
Dr. Mohamed Kassas

Preface xi

Acknowledgments xiii

Map of Wadi El Gemal National Park xiv

Map of the Main Basins of Wadi El Gemal National Park xvi

Introduction 1
- Site Description 1
  - Geomorphology 4
  - Climate 6
  - Water Resources and Hydrogeological Aspects 7
  - Ecological Features, Flora, and Vegetation 8
- Land-use and Plants 11
  - The Ababda and Land-use 11
  - Plant Communities Recognized in WGNP 14
  - Classification of Plant Uses 19

Directory of Wadi El Gemal Plants 25

Glossary 141

List of Plants by Abbadi Name 147

Plant Families and Species Identified in WGNP 152

References 157

Foreword

Dr. Mohamed Kassas

It is a pleasure to welcome the publication of this survey of plant life in what is one of Egypt's most spectacular national parks. The Wadi El Gemal National Park includes the wadi (drainage system), associated mountain formations, and stretches of coastal desert and littoral marshes. The area encompasses a wide variety of habitat types.

The Red Sea coastal chain of mountains forms a regional water-divide: short wadis that drain eastward to the Sea and long wadis that drain westward across the expanse of the Eastern Desert and flow toward the Nile Valley. Wadi El Gemal and Wadi Araba (at the northern part of the Red Sea region) are special cases that drain extensive stretches of the Eastern Desert and flow toward the Red Sea. As elsewhere in arid lands, geomorphology acts as an effective ecological driver. Landform determines the re-distribution of water resources: low-lying sites receive a generous share of water from their catchments; the area of catchment determines the volume of water received. As water accumulates, it carries with it alluvial materials (silt, wadi-fill, and so on) that provide bed-sites for plant growth and room for water storage. Coastal mountain complexes may provide niches where rare plants thrive. The coastal desert and littoral zone provide habitats for a wide diversity of vegetation types.

The introduction to *Desert Plants of Egypt's Wadi El Gemal National Park* is illustrated with a number of well-chosen photographs, and provides information on the park's main geomorphological units (landforms) and surface and ground water resources, as well as on plant uses, further underlining the intimate relationships between people and nature in the park.

The heart of the book provides botanical descriptions, notes on uses, ecological features, and distribution maps for 117 plant species out of 140 recorded in Wadi El Gemal National Park. The text is succinct and informative and the photographs invaluable.

Appendices include a glossary of terms, a table of plant names, and a table of the plants categorized by family, showing one aspect of the park's biodiversity.

The Wadi El Gemal National Park has become one of the main ecotouristic attractions of the Egyptian Red Sea coast. *Desert Plants of Egypt's Wadi El Gemal National Park* will be an invaluable companion to all visitors, who can benefit enormously from familiarizing themselves with the plants, their identities, and their diverse habitats. I look forward to seeing more illustrated guidebooks of this caliber on animal life and on other nature reserves in Egypt.

Tamer Mahmoud is to be thanked for his initiative and diligence in writing this book, as are all those who encouraged, helped, and supported him in producing it.

Preface

I will never forget my first night in the desert. It was a moonless night and I was unable to sleep because I kept hearing a strange sound outside my tent. I was terrified. Every horror movie I had ever watched came into my head. But before sunrise I discovered that the cause of my fear was the sound of sand motion and wind. After several further trips, I became accustomed to this sound and indeed came to adore the desert.

The flora of Egypt includes more than 2,300 species, in localities that vary in soil type and prevailing climatic and other environmental conditions. Habitat diversity encourages the growth of a wide range of plant species. In addition, many plants have been successfully introduced to and have acclimatized in Egypt. The plant resources, despite the general climatic aridity, are diverse and some of them provide practical resources for indigenous populations. Numerous plant species collected from the field are sold in the *attarin*, or herb stores.

However, the local culture, which is related to vegetation, is gradually being lost, due to the adoption of modern life styles and the tourism development of the last few decades. Aridity has also increased over recent decades: the last flood was in 2004 after ten dry years, reducing grazing activity and the contact between people and vegetation. Many local people have left the desert and their grazing activities to migrate to the coast to find new sources of income and educational opportunities for their children, with the result that the new generations do not care about their ancestors' culture.

At the beginning of our work in Wadi El Gemal, we organized a patrol program to discover and control the park boundaries. During these patrols I was surprised by the plant cover and diversity in the park. However, the intimate contact between those living in the area, and especially the real desert dwellers, surprised me even more:

the vegetation in Wadi El Gemal National Park and the socioeconomic relationship between plants and those who occupy the area deserve documentation, conservation, and publicity.

It took me about three years of field and office work to complete this book, including 165 field trips of between one and three days per trip. In these we surveyed more than twenty-five main wadis and their tributaries. In every location we recorded a GPS (Global Positioning System) point, preserved botanic specimens, took general photographs of the area to help us in the identification of plant community and habitat type, then close-up photographs to help us with actual plant identification. We talked with the inhabitants about their relationship with the plants and learned which ones were of real significance to them.

Back in the office, we collected numerous references about the plants of the Red Sea coast, the Eastern Desert, ecology, and plant uses. These references relate to Egypt or other parts of the world that have similar environmental and cultural conditions, such as North Africa, India, and Pakistan. In the office we also downloaded photographs and GPS points. Incidentally, I learned about GIS (Geographical Information System) programs with the specific aim of making accurate distribution maps.

In small villages like Abu Ghusun and Hamata we held meetings with Ababda shaykhs, youths, and even children, and we obtained recordings of meetings with old women through our local guards because they do not talk easily to strangers; you have to have patience to gain Ababda trust.

New horizons were opened up when escorting many leading botanists and ecologists such as Prof. Kassas and Prof. Abd El Raof Mostafa, during their visits to the park, and I learned new concepts for the interpretation of different phenomena.

After these years of field work I have a collection of about seven thousand photographs representing all seasons, stages of plant life (germination, flowering, fruiting, decline), and habitat types.

Moreover, on every trip I find a new gift, whether a plant, a stage of plant life, a place that I had never seen, or perhaps a better photograph than one I already had, or new information from the countrymen or women.

Acknowledgments

First and foremost, I would like to thank Dr. Mostafa Fouda, Director of the Nature Conservation Sector (NCS) and Dr. Mahmoud Hanafy, General Advisor of Red Sea Parks, for their support from start to finish of this work.

This book could not have been written without the encouragement and help provided by Mr. Mohammed Gad, former manager of Wadi El Gemal National Park, who has been my real teacher.

Faragalla Saad (the leader of the guards and one of the best guides I have encountered), Hassan Ahmadany, and Mohammed Ali Abdel Qader (local community guards) taught me many desert secrets. I would like to thank all my Park colleagues, especially Mohammed 'Abbas, Fahem Rezq, Mohammed Eid, Mohamed Ali, Sayed Khodary, and Mohamed Besar. Dr. Sherif Bahaa-Eddin, Usama Fathallah, and Dr. Metwaly Shabanah gave me valuable ideas for the plan of the book. My friends Dr. Abdullah Abdel Azeem and Mr. Amr Yousef gave me essential help with medical terms, subject references, and Information Technology matters.

Professor Mohamed Kassas, former president of the International Union for the Conservation of Nature (IUCN), revised the text and corrected the language, a great honor both for the book and its author.

I express my appreciation to my father and my mother, who gave me great material and moral support. My grateful thanks also to my wife, who helped me with translation, deciphered research material, and managed my schedule. Many thanks to my daughters Nada and Salma, who missed a lot of time with their father while this work was being completed.

Wadi El Gemal National Park

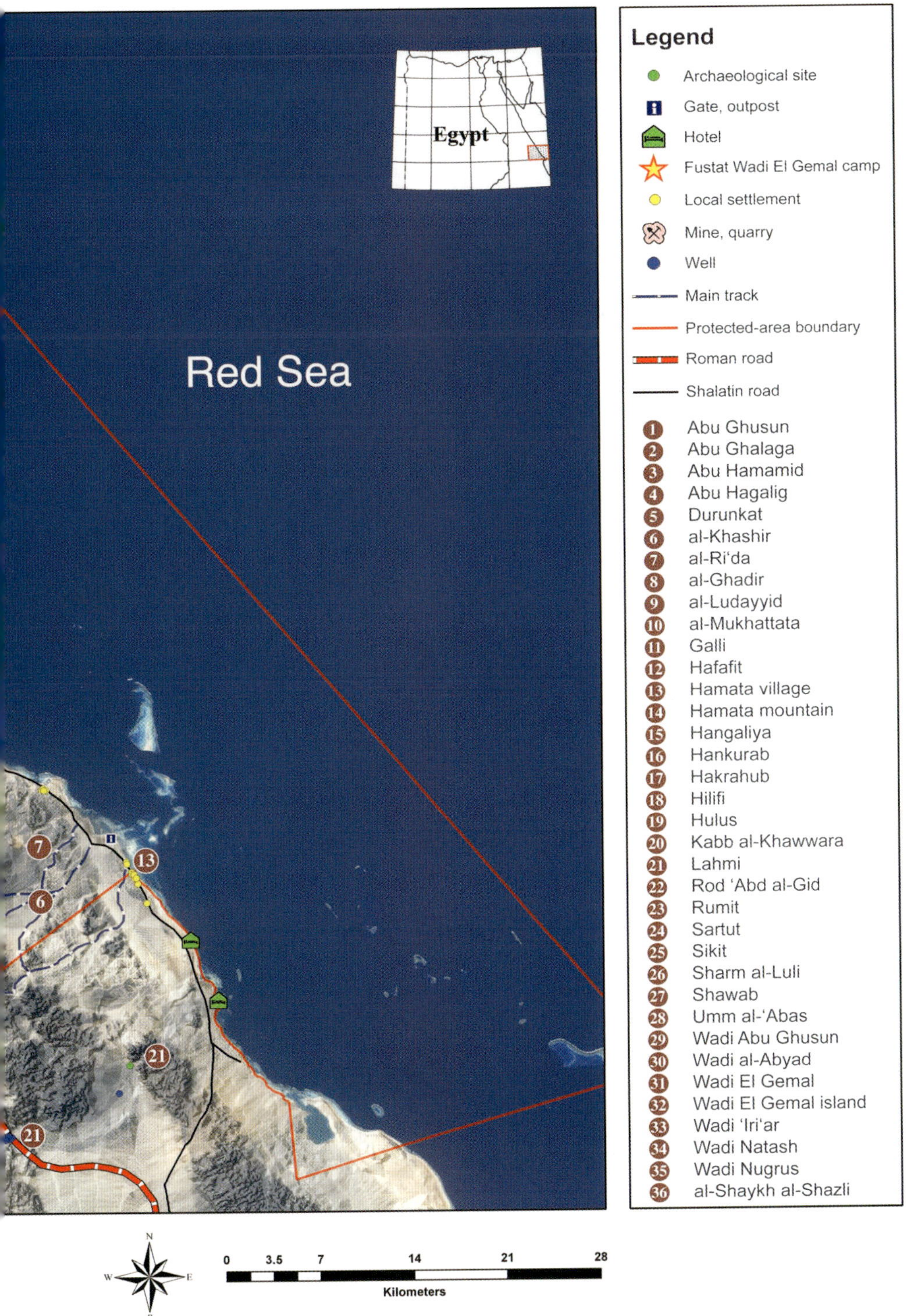
Egypt
Red Sea
7
13
6
21
21
Legend
Archaeological site
Gate, outpost
Hotel
Fustat Wadi El Gemal camp
Local settlement
Mine, quarry
Well
Main track
Protected-area boundary
Roman road
Shalatin road
1 Abu Ghusun
2 Abu Ghalaga
3 Abu Hamamid
4 Abu Hagalig
5 Durunkat
6 al-Khashir
7 al-Ri‘da
8 al-Ghadir
9 al-Ludayyid
10 al-Mukhattata
11 Galli
12 Hafafit
13 Hamata village
14 Hamata mountain
15 Hangaliya
16 Hankurab
17 Hakrahub
18 Hilifi
19 Hulus
20 Kabb al-Khawwara
21 Lahmi
22 Rod ‘Abd al-Gid
23 Rumit
24 Sartut
25 Sikit
26 Sharm al-Luli
27 Shawab
28 Umm al-‘Abas
29 Wadi Abu Ghusun
30 Wadi al-Abyad
31 Wadi El Gemal
32 Wadi El Gemal island
33 Wadi ‘Iri‘ar
34 Wadi Natash
35 Wadi Nugrus
36 al-Shaykh al-Shazli
N
W
E
S
0
3.5
7
14
21
28
Kilometers

Main basins of Wadi El Gemal National Park

Legend
Gate and outpost
Common track
Highway
Park boundary
Watershed
Red Sea
N
W
E
S
0
3.75
7.5
15
22.5
30
Kilometers

Introduction

Site Description

Egypt has declared its commitment to enhancing environmental quality and to the promotion of the sustainable use of its natural resources as a strategic choice for the nation's future. This strategy calls for the establishment and maintenance of a representative network of protected areas in the country. As part of Egypt's drive toward rational and sustainable use of its natural resources, in January 2003 the prime minister, Atef Ebeid, declared Wadi El Gemal a national park, making it the twenty-fourth national park to be declared in Egypt up to that date. Wadi El Gemal National Park (WGNP) comprises an area of 4,770 km^2 of land, in addition to about 2,000 km^2 of marine waters. The rangers' station, main entrance, and the visitor center of the park are about 335 km south of Hurghada and 45 km south of Marsa Alam.

WGNP includes unique terrestrial and marine components. The terrestrial component encompasses a substantial segment of the Red Sea hills and coastal desert. Wadi El Gemal and its delta are the focal attraction of the Park, which encompasses the entire watershed of the wadi. However, the Park includes other adjacent desert and marine habitats, which complement the wadi, both ecologically and functionally (that is, in terms of representing a meaningful management unit).

Wadi El Gemal itself is the third largest wadi in the Eastern Desert, draining into the Red Sea, and one of the better-vegetated wadis, with an estimated watershed area of some 1,476.7 km^2. The wadi watershed includes the northern flanks of Jabal Hamata in the south, as well as the southern flanks of Jabal Nugrus in the north. The Park encompasses several other important wadis, such as Wadi Abu Ghusun, Wadi al-Ranga, and Wadi al-Ri'da. Several important mountain peaks are included, such as Jabal Hamata, Jabal Nugrus, Jabal Hafafit, Jabal Hamamid, Jabal Sartut, and Jabal Sikit.

In the field, local community guards are the backbone of the work.

The shores of the region are heterogeneous in nature, encompassing rocky, sandy, and muddy beaches. The Park's coastline is about 120 km long, and has several important landmarks, such as the headlands of Ras Bughdadi and Ras Hankurab, Sharm al-Luli, and Kira‘ al-Hirtway bay.

The marine component of the Park comprises a strip of marine waters of an average width of 15 km. This component includes all the important coral reefs in the region, as well as five islands. The Hamata archipelago is made up of four islands, Wadi El Gemal Island, plus several minute sandy islets.

The best meal you can have is under a Sayyal tree after a day's field work

Escorting the leading ecologist Professor Kassas, whose remarks opened up new horizons of thought for me.

Geomorphology

The area of the Park that lies in the Eastern Desert, which is a mountainous desert landscape, forms part of the mountain range that runs parallel to the coast of the Red Sea and is made up of igneous or metamorphic rocks rising gradually from west to east. An extensive system of wadis dissects these mountains. Wadis flowing from the mountains to the Red Sea are relatively short, steep, and more numerous compared with those draining westward into the Nile Valley. Wadis may extend from the foothills to the coastal front, as do Wadi El Gemal, Wadi al-Ghadir, and Wadi al-Ranga, or may not reach the coast, such as the wadis Hulus, Nugrus, and Shawab.

Within this context, the Park can be divided into three major units:

- The coastal plain and the Red Sea coast, which comprise several different geologic features, such as rift shoulder, fault scarp, alluvial fans, piedmont plains, and raised beaches;
- The coastal hilly area and lower mountains, which form conspicuous topographical features between the coast and the main Red Sea highlands;
- The high Red Sea mountains, a huge, elongated high mountain block that forms the divide between the watersheds of wadis flowing westward to the Nile basin and those flowing eastward to the Red Sea.

Jabal Hamata and the wadis originating from the foot of the mountain.

Mountains

The inland part of the park is composed essentially of high and rugged mountains, forming a series of mountain ranges, more or less coherently trending parallel to the coast and interrupted by a number of detached masses and peaks. The highest peaks are concentrated in the southwest corner where they rise to elevations of up to 1,975 m (Jabal Hamata). The Nile basin–Red Sea divide of the area runs across the high peaks of the Red Sea Mountains with an average elevation of 650 m. Moderate relief occurs in the southeast and northwest, surrounding the high mountainous zone.

The most important hills and mountains that one can note in the Park are Hafafit (1,341 m), Nugrus (1,505 m), Z,abara (1360 m), Ghadir (864 m), Sukkari (630 m), Sikit (796 m), Ri'da (556 m), Umm Kabu (644 m), Abu Had (663 m), Misurab (1021 m), Abu Itl (643 m), Umm Suwayyih (748 m), Shawab (762 m), Kabb al-Ahmar (604 m), Umm al-'Abas (660 m), Tarafawi (1,361 m), Sartut (1,368 m), Hamata (1,975 m), Qul'an (376 m), Khashir (1,562 m), Ras al-Khurit (1,658 m), and Mukhattata (570 m).

Wadis

The area is dissected by a number of wadis that originate in the mountainous terrain and mostly run toward the Red Sea, following the general eastward slope. Slope gradient is generally steep in the upper drainage reaches and tends to be gentle to the east. The wadis are mostly oriented E–W, WNW–ENE, NNW–NE. The main wadis are important as a network of tracks in the area and as the main arteries for underground water. The principal wadis of WGNP from north to south are:

Wadi al-Ri'da.

Ghadir, Zabara, Umm Lasaf, Khililat al-Bahari, Khililat al-Qibli, Sharm al-Fiqiri, ‘Iri‘ar, Ramarim, Wadi El Gemal, Hulus, Al Abyad, Tarafawi, Umm Samyuki, Ma‘rasani, Abu Itl, Durunkat, Hangaliya, Hafafit, Abu Had, Nugrus, Sikit, Mukhattata, Umm Suwayyih, Umm Hiran, Nasbiya, Umm Siyal, Umm Kabu, Ghazal, Umm al-‘Abas, Abu Ghusun, Abu Ghalga, Kabb al-Ahmar, Shawab, Rumit, Abu ‘Ushush, Hakrahub, Ranga, Hilifi, Hamata, Mastura, Jukub, Qul‘an, Ri‘da, and al-Khashir.

Coastal Plain

The coastal plain has a low topography and a variable breadth in the range of 0.6 km in the north (Wadi Ghadir)—to more than 12 km in the south at Hamata. Numerous parallel wadis drain the Red Sea rugged mountains and flow to the coastal plain. Sedimentary systems from the piedmont to the Red Sea coast comprise alluvial fans, wadis and littoral (reef) terraces. Modern fringing coral reefs, 50–100 m wide, extend along the coast, though they are lacking at the mouths of some of the larger wadis as a result of sediment (sand and pebbles) deposits during floods. Protected anchorages for small boats, or *marsa*s, are found at the mouths of some wadis.

Islands

There are five islands in WGNP. Wadi El Gemal Island is located 5 km off Ras Bughdadi at the north end of the Park. Extending northeast from Hamata is the Qul‘an Archipelago—sometimes called the Hamata Islands. The archipelago consists of four islands: from north to south, Siyal, Shawarit, Umm al-Shaykh, and Mahabis Islands. A fifth, small island lies off the Hamata mangrove, which is periodically connected with the mainland at low tide. The islands range from 3 to 7 km from the mainland. They are low-lying with sandy beaches and raised fossil reefs, with fossilized coral and carbonate rocks. The entire region around the islands is a shallow water area with rugged bottom morphology, and is surrounded by well-developed shallow fringing coral reefs bordered by a sloping sandy bed. Beyond the shallow reef-flats and intertidal areas the reef slope drops away and is replaced by sand, sand with seagrass, or sand with coral patches.

Climate

Wadi El Gemal National Park falls within latitudes N 24° 5’ and N 24° 53’. It is part of a hyper-arid region with hot, rainless summers and mild winters. Precipitation falls mainly in the fall and winter months, but is not an annual event; rather, it is episodic and localized, often received in the form of short, heavy downpours that cause flash flooding. The average annual precipitation is about 17.4 mm, at Ras Banas meteorological station. The maximum amount of precipitation recorded in one day was 64 mm, on 24 November 1966. The monthly mean temperature varies between 24 and

Wadi El Gemal Island.

38°C during summer and 12 and 26°C during winter. Relative humidity varies between 28 percent in summer and 57 percent in winter. The average evapotranspiration rate varies between 8.7 mm/day in winter and 28 mm/day in summer.

Over much of the year northwesterly winds predominate; only rarely do southern winds occur. The wind velocity ranges between 0.129 km/h and 66.07 km/h, with an average of 22.04 km/h in summer, and between 0.096 km/h and 62.93 km/h, with an average of 19.26 km/h in winter (Meteorological Station, Institute Oceanography and Fisheries, Red Sea branch). In general, wind velocity is distinctly higher during the day, a phenomenon that can be explained by higher temperature differences between the heated landmass and cool seawater during the day.

Water Resources and Hydrogeological Aspects

Water resources in WGNP depend on the rainfall and groundwater supplies. The groundwater of the region is supported mainly by precipitation, and depends upon the slope of the ground surface, the different rock dykes, and the rate of rains and floods.

Drainage Basins

Along the Red Sea coast flash floods represent a rare natural but ecologically important phenomenon. The area is occasionally subjected to heavy showers during winter, followed by torrential floods, which may damage roads and displace structures. Twenty-three drainage basins with outlets on the Red Sea have been identified in the area between Marsa Alam and Ras Banas (Mansour 2003). They range between small (11.52 km^2) and large (1,476.7 km^2) in area. The drainage network is well-developed and fairly dense but not consistent across the whole area. Wadi Ghadir and Wadi al-Ri'da have high relief and ruggedness and this produces a fast runoff concentration, with a corresponding high probability of flooding. Wadi El Gemal has the highest maximum runoff, followed by Wadi Lahmi and Wadi Ghadir. This explains the good vegetative cover of these drainage basins. In contrast, the basins of Wadi Ranga and Wadi Umm al-'Abas can be classified as less flourishing.

Groundwater and Wells *(Birs)*

The groundwater resources in the Eastern Desert wadis originate mainly from occasional rainfall that infiltrates the friable loose sediments and accumulates in basement depressions, or is trapped by faults and buried dykes. Groundwater quality has been investigated in the three main wells of Wadi El Gemal basin (Bir Wadi El Gemal, Bir Umm Ghanam, and Bir Hafafit) (Ahmed, 2001). The salinity of groundwater varies from one year to another, as well as from one season to another: but average salinity was 490 ppm at Bir Umm Ghannam, 960 ppm at Bir Wadi El Gemal, and 3185 ppm at Bir Hafafit in August 2000.

Moreover, the water of the area is slightly alkaline, the pH value ranging from 7.38 at Bir Wadi El Gemal to 7.83 at Bir Umm Ghanam. Total Dissolved Solids (TDS) and the hardness of the collected water samples from Bir Umm Ghannam and Bir Wadi El Gemal are mostly lower than the World Health Organization (WHO) (1984) maximum permissible limits for drinking water. TDS and hardness of the water samples from Bir Hafafit were above the WHO (1984) maximum.

The Last Flood

The last flood was in November 2004, after ten rainless years. It rained in the hills and wadis of al-Abyad, Hulus, Durunkat, Gali, Abu Hamamid, and on the western part of Wadi El Gemal. Finally it accumulated a flood of moderate strength along Wadi El Gemal. It took two days to drain into the sea. In addition, it rained on the regions of Lahmi, al-Khashir, al-Ri'da, Hilifi, Hangaliya, Abu Ghusun, and Hafafit, but not enough to cause a flood.

Ecological Features, Flora, and Vegetation

As WGNP belongs to the arid desert, plant growth is mostly confined to the drainage systems which collect and contain runoff water, bringing with it alluvial deposits. The plant life includes two principal growth forms: ephemerals and perennials. Ephemerals are almost exclusively dependent on rainfall, whereas the perennials may exploit moisture stored in subsurface layers of the soil.

Sartout springs.

Bir Amira in Wadi Rumit, about 25 m deep.

The last flood deep in Wadi El Gemal, more than 30 km in from the coast.

In terms of flora, Kassas (1953) classified the Wadi El Gemal–Hamata Area as a part of the "Southern (Nubian) Section" of the Eastern Desert. The complexity of WGNP's mountainous area produces a similarly complex set of habitat conditions. In the mountains, arboreal vegetation, that is, *Acacia tortilis* and *Balanites aegyptiaca*, grow and predominate (for example, Zahran and Willis, 2009). Other common trees include *Tamarix aphylla* and *T. nilotica*. Barakat (2003) reported that the flora of WGNP comprises 93 plant species of which 72 are perennials and 21 are ephemerals. Zahran and Willis (1992) and Barakat (2003) recognized the floral communities in WGNP: mangrove, salt marsh, coastal dunes, reed swamp, coastal plain, down stream vegetation, wadi vegetation, plateau, and the mountain community.

Land-use and Plants

The Ababda and Land-use

The area encompassed an important segment of the historical trans-desert trade routes between Bernice and Edfu, with the result that its inhabitants varied greatly over the past twenty-five centuries. Roman, Ptolemaic, and Islamic monuments prove as much. Today's Ababda tribes are the main indigenous inhabitants of WGNP. They were among the first peoples to inhabit the desert between the Red Sea and the Nile River. According to some references, they are descendants of Begga tribes (African tribes). However, they reject this claim, and *shaykh*s ('wise men') have records that relate them to Arab tribes from the Arabian Peninsula. The Ababda have their own traditions, customs, and cultures that are different from other Eastern Desert tribes. Grazing is the prime occupation, with herds of camels, sheep, and goats. They also collect plants for food and trade. They are nomadic, always seeking areas with recent rainfall and good pasture.

The utilization of vegetation in WGNP is one of the more impressive aspects of Ababda adaptation to environmental conditions. In plants, the Ababda find a source of medicine for people and livestock, though the most extensive use of plants is for grazing goats and camels. The prominence of desert plants led the Ababda to identify many places by botanical landmarks, whether it is the abundance of a certain plant species or their unique but prominent presence. For example, Wadi Abu Ghusun means 'that has many twigs,' Abu Itl, 'that has tamarisk,' Umm Lasaf, 'that has capparis,' Abu Hagalig, 'that has Balanitis,' and Umm Sayyal, 'that contains Acacia.'

Ababda men during a celebration day (Bayt al-Ababda opening day). Sword dancing is a major part of their celebrations.

A woman from the Ababda tribe designs a local traditional mat *(farsh)*.

A local traditional shelter (*borsh*)

Grazing; an image of a woman working.

Their dwellings are small temporary structures called *borsh*. Houses are built of branches and covered with cloth and wool, on relatively high ground at the wadi edge to avoid contact with sudden floods. Women participate in essential activities, such as house-building, fishing, and grazing, and they are very expert in handicrafts.

The Ababda look to their *shaykh*s and tribal elders to solve their conflicts. The two conflicting sides put their case to an arbitration council and leave the final decision to them. The council declares the decision at the end of the session. The judgment usually rules that the guilty party give up a certain number of camels, other valuables, or money.

There are some two thousand Ababda in WGNP, concentrated in Abu Ghusun, Hamata, al-Shaykh al-Shazli, Qul'an, Shawab, Rumit, Hafafit, and Abu Ghalaga. They are divided into main families like the Kergab, Geregab, Harranab, Oqada, Teman, Nofaa, Zidab, Balalab, and Fehedab.

The nature of their work depends on location, with those who live near the coast working mostly in fishing, tourism, or in mining, and those who live in wadis working in grazing and mining. Nowadays they have new job opportunities as park guards, guides for safari tourists, and as workers in WGNP infrastructure activity such as the establishment of tracks, outposts, and the building of gates.

Ababda child.

Plant Communities Recognized in WGNP

Mangrove

Climatic conditions and shoreline morphology in the coastal part of WGNP allow the growth of mangrove trees, which are confined to small sheltered bays cut into the beach. *Avicennia marina* forms monotypic bushy forests. Another species, *Rhizophora mucronata*, grows on the Red Sea coast further south, beyond the park boundaries.

Salt Marsh

Saline lands are widely distributed globally and represent about 10 percent of the earth's terrestrial surface (O'Leary and Glenn, 1994). In the Park, distinct zones are evident within the littoral plant communities corresponding to their levels of salinity tolerance. The salt marshes communities often fringe mangroves on the coast and their extension inland depends on the raised land further west. The plant cover is formed of stands of uniform growth of a single dominant species and a few associates, mainly halophytes. Thus, a mosaic of species is often recorded and varies according to local topography and soil salinity: *Arthrocnemon*, *Sarcocorina*, *Atriplex farinosa*, and *Zygophyllum album*.

Hamata mangrove.

Salt marshes community in Umm al-'Abas region.

Coastal dunes community in Sharm Sabiha.

Coastal Dunes

Further from the shoreline, distinctive vegetation can be observed growing on sand dunes, forming phytogenic mounds or hillocks. *Tamarix* mounds are perhaps the most prominent among these, but there are several other species growing within this type of ecosystem, such as *Aeluropus lagopoides*, *Limonium axillare*, *Zygophyllum album, Zygophyllum coccineum, Tamarix aphylla*, and *Tamarix nilotica*.

Reed Swamp

Reed swamps are present where there is seepage of fresh or brackish water onto the surface. The large swamp at the mouth of Wadi El Gemal (the Wadi El Gemal delta) holds the only example of a reed swamp over much of the Egyptian Red Sea. This special condition has led to the development of a peculiar floristic assemblage, characterized by the presence of reeds but also some halophytes in addition to palms. The swampy areas are dominated by reeds: *Phragmites australis*, and *Cyperus* sp. The delta of Wadi El Gemal also harbors other species, the most notable being: *Avicennia marina, Tamarix aphylla, Tamarix nilotica, Zygophyllum album, Zygophyllum coccineum, Limonium axillare, Hyphaene thebaica* (Dom-palm), and *Phoenix dactylifera* (Date-palm).

Coastal Plain

This extends from the littoral area to the foot of the coastal mountains and is characterized by the semi-halophytics *Limonium axillare* and *Zygophyllum coccineum*, as well as small thickets of *Tamarix aphylla*, *T. nilotica*, and *Salvadora persica*, and the smaller herbaceous *Zilla spinosa* and *Pulicaria undulata.*

Reed swamp community in Wadi El Gemal Delta.

Al-Ghadir coastal plain community.

Downstream Vegetation

The littoral downstream of wadis supports vegetation in the intermediate area between the coastal desert plain and the main wadi vegetation and varies according to the geomorphology and soil characteristics. The eastern part, closer to the coast, where the soil is sandy and saline, usually supports a range from halophytic to xerophytic species with *Zygophyllum album*, *Z. coccineum*, *Tamarix aphylla*, and *Tamarix nilotica*.

Wadi Vegetation

The main trunks of wadis are dominated by *Acacia tortilis* subsp. *tortilis*; *A. tortilis* subsp. *raddiana*; and *Balanites aegyptiaca* (as in Wadi El Gemal). Associates are *Acacia ehrenbergiana* (which sometimes replaces *A. tortilis*), *Panicum turgidum*, *Leptadenia pyrotechnica, Capparis deciduas, Lycium shawii, Aerva javanica, Solenostemma arghel, Citrullus colocynthis*, and *Ochradenus baccatus*. Chasmophytes such as *Capparis spinosa* grow in rock crevices along the wadi sides (but also upstream of wadis, as in Wadi Umm Lassaf). A *Maerua crassifolia* tree was a rare find, associated with *Acacia ehrenbergiana, Panicum turgidum, Cleome droserifolia, Trichodesma africanum* as the upstream area of Wadi Hulus.

The following list includes other plants recorded in the main stream of various wadis within WGNP: *Caylusea* sp., *Chrozophora tinctoria*, *Citrullus colocynthis*, *Erodium* sp., *Fagonia* sp., *Heliotropium* sp., *Launaea* sp., *Lindenbergia indica*, *Lotus* sp., *Pulicaria undulata, Senna alexandrina*, *Tephrosia aegyptiaca, Trichodesma africanum, Zilla spinosa, Zygophyllum simplex*, and *Zygophyllum coccineum*.

Wadi vegetation community (Wadi al-Abyad).

Mountain vegetation (Hamata hills).

Mountain

This community inhabits mountains that face the Red Sea and reach over 900 m in height. It is characterized by examples of *Moringa peregrina*, *Ficus palmata*, *Lindenbergia indica*, and *Kickxia* sp. Several rare species are recorded here, including *Acacia etbaica, Rhus tripartite*, and *Adiantum capillus-veneris.*

Classification of Plant Uses

The vegetation of WGNP is of considerable economic importance to local people. The vegetation of the dry land they inhabit provides food, shelter, health, recreation, and even kitchen tools. We can classify the utilization of plant resources as follows:

Grazing and Forage for Livestock

The majority of WGNP local people are employed in grazing, so the exploitation of desert vegetation ranks as the most significant aspect of land use. Rainfall, and hence annual plant growth, unpredictable, both in time and location, is found only in a limited area for a limited time. Pastoral nomads move with their livestock to the places where rain has fallen, in order to take advantage of the short-lived ephemerals. In rainless periods, which occur seasonally but can extend up to ten years, woody perennial plants provide the main food for the nomads' livestock.

Grazing is the main use of plants in WGNP. Camels graze on *Tamarix aphylla*.

Animals, both domestic and wild, can graze on about 130 of the species growing in WGNP. Among the most palatable of these are Leguminosaea. But the most available plant is *Zilla spinosa*. Observations and interviews with WGNP inhabitants indicated a selective use of plants by animals. The camel's diet is of a wider variety than other domestic animals. *Tamarix nilotica* is apparently good for camels and goats, but not for sheep, while *Aerva javanica* is a preferred diet for gazelles. *Lycium shawii* is a fast-growing plant but local people do not allow their animals to graze it in the first month after rain because it is poisonous then. Nor do local people allow their animals to graze *Crotalaria microphylla* before sunrise, because they believe that it is very harmful. The green *Crotalaria aegyptiaca* is grazed by camels and gazelles, but is poisonous to sheep and goats.

In this context we can divide the range plants into two groups. The first comprises the perennial plants that form the permanent but limited source of food for wild and domestic animals: *Acacia* spp., *Balanites aegyptiaca*, and *Tamarix nilotica* are the main members of this group. The availability of this group may extend to ten years without water supplied by floods or rain.

The second group includes ephemeral plants that provide temporary pasture for animals but are more abundant and have high nutritional content. These emerge after falls of rain, which do not necessarily occur every year. This group comprises about sixty-three species in WGNP. All of them can be grazed, but the most well-known members of this group are *Lotononis platycarpa*, *Astragalus vogelii*, *Astragalus eremophilus, Neurada procumbens*. Some members of this group can survive for two or three years and thus provide additional food resources for animals; *Tephrosia purpurea* and *Zilla spinosa* are examples.

Fuel

Although all desert shrubs, trees, and woody perennials can be cut for fuel, local people usually use only dry branches and dead plants. But the non-locals in the desert act differently. They may be travelers, workers in the mines, or other transients. They cut green plants when they cannot find dry ones. Cutting live wood reduces the availability of plants for grazing and causes erosion. In this context, we should mention that local people are divided into two groups according to their use of plants as fuel. The first comprises those who live near the coastline. This group is quite advanced in using alternative fuel resources such as Kerosene and gas stoves. They only use plants as fuel to make *gabori* and *rodaf* (traditional types of bread). They also use dead branches to make *salat* (traditional meat dish) and *gabana* (traditional coffee). The second group of local people consists of those who live in wadis away from the coast. They use dry plants as fuel in all activities, including for heat and cooking. The best plants used by local people as fuel are *Acacia* spp. because they produce a better-quality fire for longer and relatively fewer fumes than other plants. They also add any dry herbs, mainly *Zilla spinosa*, to enhance burning.

Using branches for fuel. Above: cooking *jabana*; Left: preparing *gabori*.

Plant uses—clockwise from top left: camel saddles; *jabana* container; combs; containers for domestic use.

Timber

Timber trees are important to local people because they are used for building houses, shades, and some parts of boats. *Borsh*, the local traditional tent, is built by using the stems and branches of Acacia trees. The wood of *Balanites aegyptiaca* is used for making camel saddles and kitchen tools because it is hard and light. The use of plants for timber is very limited in WGNP, however. Local people very rarely cut living trees, preferring to keep them for grazing, and rely only on dead trees.

Charcoal-making

Before the declaration of the Wadi El Gemal region as a national park, charcoal production was one of the few traditional cash products available to inhabitants. This is a process by which the wood, mostly from Acacia trees, is transformed into charcoal through anaerobic combustion. Traditionally, only dead trees and branches were used for charcoal production; however, because of increased economic demands on local people and a shrinking resource base, live branches or even whole trees were cut down to provide for charcoal-making. Most of the charcoal was transported to the Nile Valley and tourist resorts for use in water-pipe smoking. The activity was widespread in the region, but is now extremely limited as a result of law enforcement (specifically Law No. 102 of 1983 relating to activities in national parks) and because of the job opportunities, both temporary and permanent, now available to local people.

Medicinal use

Seventy plant species in WGNP are of known medicinal value (Mahmoud 2009). These include herbs (twenty-six species), perennial herbs (eight species), shrubs (twenty-three species), and trees (thirteen species). Medicinal plants are distributed throughout the different habitats recognized in WGNP. The wadi habitat includes 59.2 percent of the recorded medicinal plants, the coastal plain, 18.4 percent, the mountains, 17.1 percent, and the littoral habitat, 5.2 percent. About 29 percent of plant medicinal uses are commonly employed in the park, and 71 percent of the medicinal uses are recorded out of the park, that is, in other regions within Egypt or abroad, mainly in Asia (India, China, and Pakistan) or Africa (Tunisia, Tanzania, Sahara, Morocco, and Cape Verde). Some of these uses are theoretical and have not yet been applied in practice.

Numerous medicinal plants are found in desert areas. The plant resources, despite the climatic aridity, are diverse and some of them provide food or remedies for the native inhabitants. Many plant species are collected from the field to be sold in *attarin,* or herb stores. Local people currently do not collect all species of known medicinal value. Among those regularly collected, the more important are: *Citrullus colocynthis*, *Senna alexandrina*, *Solenostemma arghel*, *Salvadora persica*, *Balanites aegyptiaca*, *Capparis spinosa*, and *Cleome droserifolia*.

Food

About thirty species of WGNP plants have edible parts. These plants may be eaten fresh, cooked, dried, or pickled. Local people eat the fruits of *Ficus palmata, Balanites aegyptica*, *Phoenix dactylifera*, *Glossonema boveanum*, *Salvadora persica*, and *Capparis decidua*. They use the grains of *Panicum turgidum*. The leaves of *Rumex vesicarius*, *Asphodelus tenuifolius,* Malva *parviflora*, and *Launaea capitata* are eaten or cooked. The flowers of some plants such as *Acacia tortilis* are edible. In addition, some plants are used as flavors or drinks, such as *Pulicaria incisa.*

Other Uses

These include the production of oil and fiber, and the use of plants for tanning leather *(Acacia ehrenbergiana)* and in making mats, ropes, and baskets *(Juncus rigidus)*. Shrubs and trees are important in making shades and hedges, and for their role in soil stabilization. Plants, particularly those of the Leguminosaea family, also play a vital role in nitrogen enrichment of soil by hosting nitrogen fixation microorganisms.

Directory of Wadi El Gemal Plants

Introduction

To date, 140 plant species belonging to 44 plant families have been recorded in WGNP, and we expect that there are more species, but we need both rain and further surveys. The most represented families are Leguminosae, with eighteen species including nine perennials, eight annuals, and one short-lived perennial. The next best represented are Compositae, with nine species that include four perennials, four annuals, and one short-lived perennial. The rarest families are Adiantaceae, represented by one perennial *(Adiantum capillus-veneris)* and Niyctaginaceae, with one perennial herb *(Commicarpus helenae)*. The most common species recorded are *Acacia tortilis*, *Balanites aegyptiaca*, *Tamarix nilotica*, *Lycium shawii*, *Limonium axillare*, *Zilla spinosa*, and *Lotononis platycarpa*. The rarest species are *Hyphaene thebaica*, *Zizphus spina-christi*, *Adiantum capillus-veneris*, *Cleome amblyocarpa*, and *Salsola imbricata*.

This section documents all the information we have obtained on 117 plant species. These are arranged in alphabetical order by Latin name. Each entry features photographs of the species and the following information:

1. Scientific name and family name
2. Common English names: English name (if any)
3. Common local name: local Abbadi name (from the Ababda)
4. Other common names: other Arabic names (if any)
5. Description
6. Importance and uses: within the Park, in Egypt, and the rest of the world.
7. Ecology and distribution: within the Park
8. Distribution map: a map of the Park with green lines representing the main tracks. The red dots represent individuals of the species (at least one).

Abutilon fruticosum

Guill. and Perr. in Guill., Perr., and Rich., Fl. Senegamb. Tent. 1:70 (1831)

Common English name: Texas Indian mallow
Common local name: (Hambuk) همبوك
Description: An erect, velvety, perennial herb to shrub, up to 2 m high. Stems are branched with long white-yellow hairs. Leaves coarsely dentate, rounded cordate; stellate pubescent on both sides; pale green, with triangular acute apex. Flowers large, usually in pairs; exceptionally beautiful, shiny yellow with purple center.
Importance and uses: Grazing by both domestic and wild animals. Not recorded as having medicinal or other local economic value.
Ecology and distribution: Grows in desert and stony wadis. Not common in the Park. Recorded at Hilifi and Rumit.

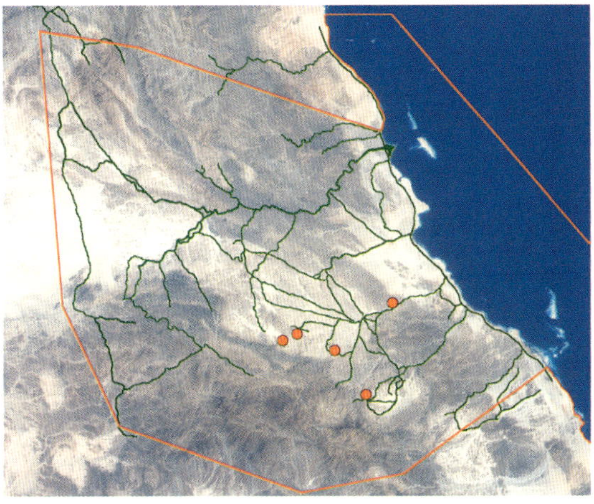

Acacia ehrenbergiana

Hayne, Getreue Darstell. Gew. 10, t, 29 (1872). (Leguminosa)

Common local name: (Salam) سلم

Description: A much-branched tall shrub or small tree. Bark green or brown, smooth, shiny, and peeling. Thorns 4–6 cm long, white, straight, set out in axillary pairs, longer than the adjacent leaves. Twigs glabrous or nearly so. Leaflets small. Flower heads globose and bright yellow. Pods bright red when young, dehiscent and narrow to linear.

Importance and uses: The wood is used for making high-quality shepherds' staves. It produces a second-rate edible gum. The bark fiber used locally for rope-making. Also browsed and used as firewood.

Ecology and distribution: Grows in sandy and stony wadis and plains. Very rare in the eastern part of the Park, but very common in the western part, especially in al-Nuhud, 'Antar, and al-Nikhira. A particularly good strip is found along the southern part of the al-Shaykh al-Shazli road.

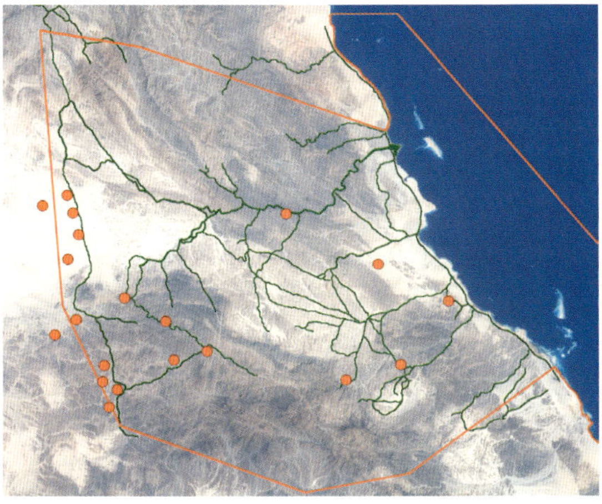

Acacia etbaica

Schweinf., Linnaea 35:330 (1868). (Leguminosa)

Common local name: ('Arad) عرض

Description: Tree or shrub 2.5–12 m tall. Trunk distinct, with flattened or rounded crown in older trees. Flowers white or cream. Pod (fruit) linear-oblong, purple-brown to red-brown, shiny, straight, often attenuated at the base and glabrous or puberulous.

Importance and uses: The dry leaves used locally for tanning hides. Provides the pillars and beams to support the heavy earthen roofs of houses. A source of firewood and also good for grazing. In other regions the bark is chewed as a stimulant and used in the treatment of gonorrhea. Right, bottom: A local Bedouin extracts dried leaves for use in tanning hides.

Ecology and distribution: Grows in stony wadis. Recorded only in the Hamata sector, especially on hills and high altitude valleys, as in the Hilifi and Hamata mountains.

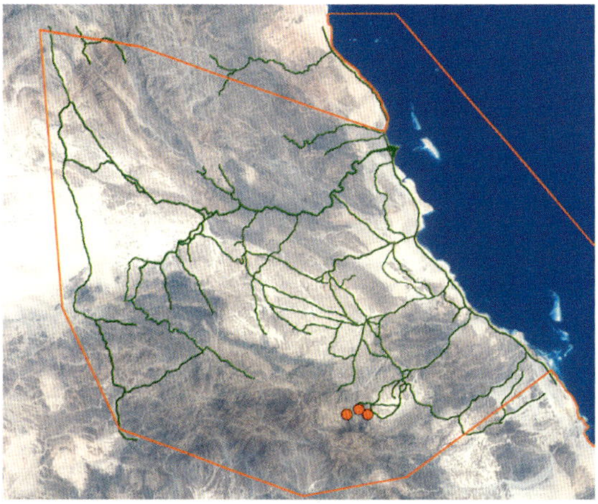

Acacia tortilis subsp. *raddiana*

(Savi) Brenan, Kew Bull. 12:87 (1957)
(Leguminosa)

Common English name: Acacia
Common local name: (Sayyal) سيال
Description: A tall spiny desert tree. Its distinctive trunk can reach one meter in diameter in older trees. Young trees have an irregular crown; older trees a broad, rounded umbrella-shaped crown. A reddish bark. Flowers whitish-yellow, arranged in heads. Sometimes flowers twice a year. Legumes flattened, spirally twisted, with several very hard seeds. Branches, leaflets, and legumes glabrous. In times of drought the tree can drop its leaves.
Importance and uses: The most useful tree for local people: excellent for firewood and fodder for livestock. In prolonged rainless periods the main source of fodder for animals. Its wood is hard and good for construction. Gum from the tree is used to treat high stomach acidity or is dissolved in water and used to treat ocular infections and jaundice. The gum is important in many industries, especially the food industry.
Ecology and distribution: A most popular plant. You will see these trees all over the Park.

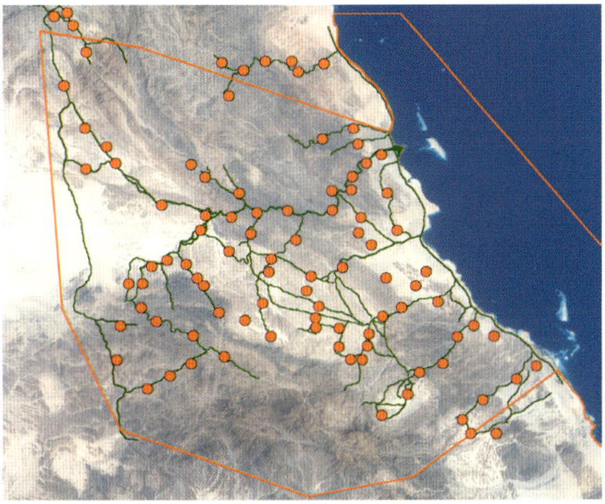

Acacia tortilis subsp. *tortilis*

(Forssk.) Hayne, Getreue Darstell. Gew. 10, t.31 (1827). (Leguminosa)

Common English name: Umbrella thorn
Common local name: (Samur) سمر
Description: A medium-sized, umbrella-shaped tree, often with several trunks from the base, reduced to a small wiry shrub under extremely arid conditions. A distinctive spreading crown. Two thorn types, long-straight and shorter-hooked. White or pale yellow fragrant flowers cluster in round heads. Flowers later develop into bunches of spirally twisted pubescent pods.
Importance and uses: Local people eat the flowers, which taste sweet. Good browsing for animals. Provides fodder throughout most of the dry season when other sources are scarce, and shade for animals and people during the hot seasons. Some of the most palatable grass species grow beneath its canopy. A good source of charcoal and firewood.
Ecology and distribution: Very resistant to drought and salinity. One of the most widespread trees in the Park. Recorded in Wadi El Gemal, Abu Ghusun, al-Ludayyid and Hulus.

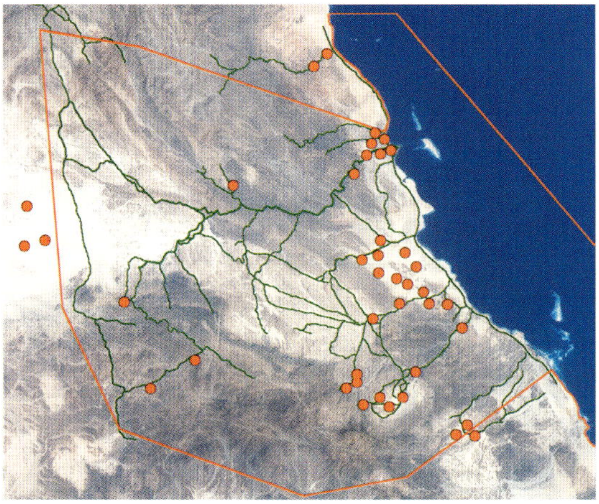

Adiantum capillus-veneris

L., 1753 (Adiantaceae)

Common English name: Avenca, Maidenhair fern
Common local name: (Kusbarat al-bir) كسبرة البئر
Description: A delicate, perennial fern (vascular plants which reproduce by spores), with a creeping rhizome. The fronds (leaves) are 5–35 cm long. The sori are arranged on the veins of the secured area of the lobes of the pinnules.
Importance and uses: This plant has no obvious local use, perhaps due to its rarity. But across the world it is one of the most famous medicinal herbs, used for asthma, chest colds, cough, edema, flu, and urinary disorders.
Ecology and distribution: Grows in moist habitats rich in organic matter, usually on the moist walls of wells and springs of fresh water, as in Sartut.

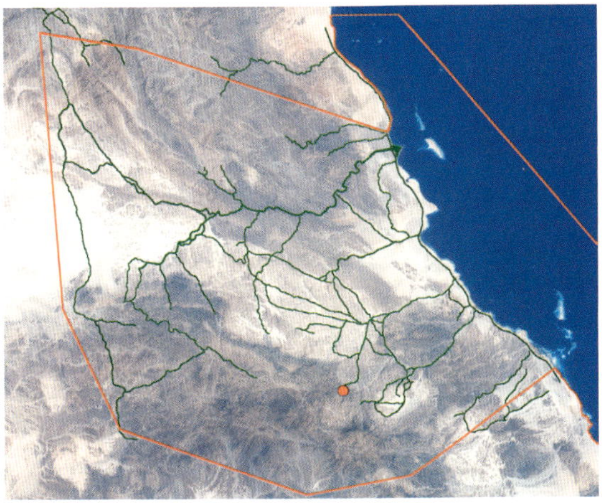

Aeluropus lagopoides

(L.) Trin., 1864 (Gramineae)

Common local name: (Dahasir) دهاسير

Description: A creeping perennial grass. Culms (stems) ascending, or prostrate, 5–30 cm long. Leaves cauline and distichous. Leaf-sheaths loose and open for most of their length. Leaf-blades are folded or involute, with acuminate and pungent apex. Inflorescence globose, elliptic, or oblong heads of closely crowded spikelets on long peduncles.

Importance and uses: Grazed by animals, especially in the absence of other grazing resources. No record of local medicinal or economic value.

Ecology and distribution: Grows only in highly saline soil, and a dominant plant in such habitats. It occupies a wide area in Wadi El Gemal Delta and in Sharm al-Luli.

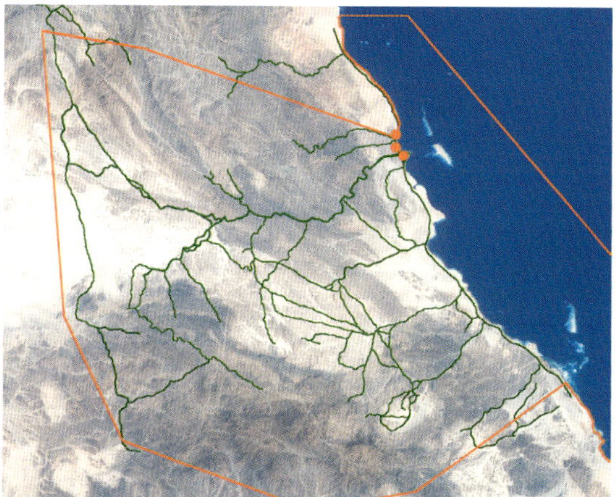

Aerva javanica

(Burm.) Juss., 1820 (Amaranthaceae)

Common English name: Desert Cotton, Kapok bush

Common local name: (Ara) أرا

Description: A white to yellowish, woolly perennial subshrub, up to 1.6 m high. A dioecious plant with more slender spikes in the male individuals. Leaves alternate, covered by hairs. The whole plant densely covered in branched and short hairs. Flowers in dense woolly spikes.

Importance and uses: Grazed by animals; local people notice it is the preferred plant of gazelles. No local medicinal value recorded, but in other regions, such as Wadi Allaqi, locals use the paste of the roots for acne-like conditions. In addition, it is believed by Bedouin that smoke from burning its leaves offers protection against the 'evil eye' and a remedy for toothache.

Ecology and distribution: Very common in the sandy wadis and desert plains. Recorded in Wadi El Gemal, Hafafit, and Abu Ghusun.

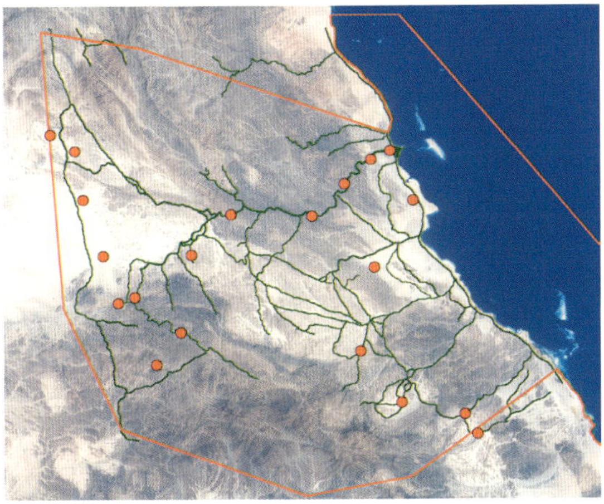

Aizoon canariense

L., 1753 (Aizonaceae)

Common English name: Horse purslane
Common local name: (Hidak) حداك
Description: A prostrate annual herb. Thick, almost woody, zigzag-curved branches. Succulent, spatulate leaves. Flowers solitary, sessile, yellow inside and in the stem forks. Seeds ribbed, black, shiny, contained in a broad five-angled capsule. (Right, top: young plant. Right, center: mature plant. Right, bottom: capsules and flowers.)
Importance and uses: A grazing herb. Locals use the dried ground leaves and tender shoots for porridge or soup. Leaves and shoots edible; eaten fresh.
Ecology and distribution: Like all ephemerals, appears after rain. Grows in sandy plains. Common in Wadi El Gemal, Abu Ghusun, and al-Ri'da.

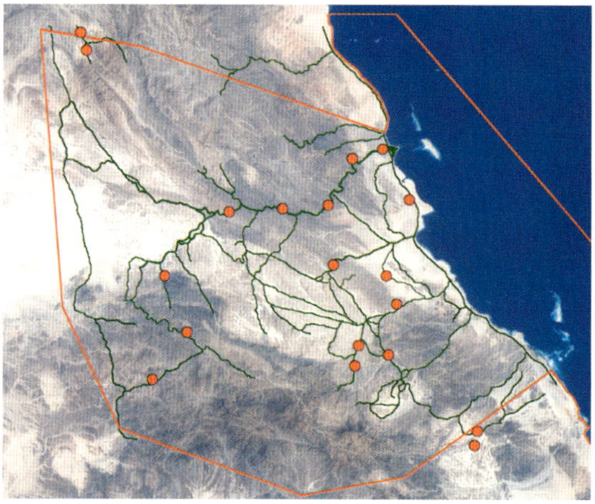

Amaranthus graecizans

L., 1753 (Amaranthaceae)

Common local name: (Lisan al-tayr) لسان الطير

Description: An erect annual herb. About 15–70 cm high. Stem green to reddish, slender to stout, angular and glabrous. Leaves broadly ovate to linear-lanceolate, petiolate, and glabrous on both surfaces. Flowers in globose axillary clusters, more male flowers in upper whorls. Seeds round, compressed and shiny, dark brown to black.

Importance and uses: Grazed by animals, especially in rainy seasons. No local medicinal or economic value.

Ecology and distribution: Grows in sandy soil. Recorded in al-Ri'da, al-Khashir, and Wadi El Gemal.

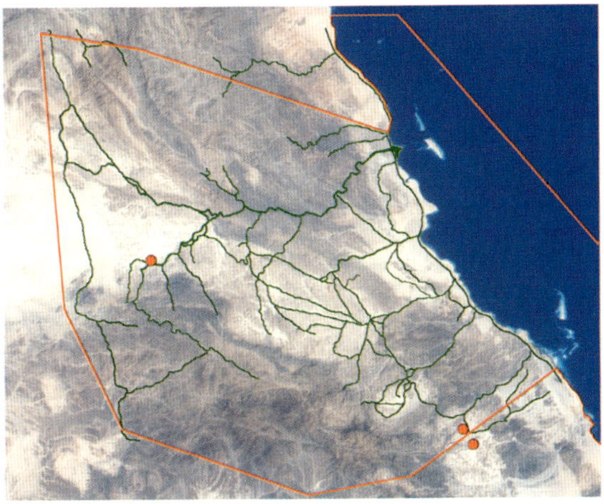

Anastatica hierochuntica

L., 1753 (Cruciferae)

Common English name: Hand of Mary, Rose of Jericho

Common local names: (Kaff Maryam) كف مريم (Umm Kammash) أمّ كمّاش

Description: An annual, small, star-shaped plant. Branched from the base, prostrate, with white flowers. Fruiting plants indurate, globose, with incurved pungent branches carrying persistent fruits. The plants roll inward after maturity to form a tight woody ball. The fruiting plants are hygroscopic, expanding their branches easily on immersing in water. Unlike the dispersal mechanisms of many desert plants, the whole dead skeleton of the plant is involved in seed dispersal and preservation. This process depends on the hygroscopic nature of the lignified conducting tissue that bends when dry and straightens under wet conditions.

Importance and uses: Popularly believed to ease childbirth when burnt as incense in the birth chamber. It has proven effects as a cardiotonic.

Ecology and distribution: Grows in wadi beds. Inconspicuous and short-lived when green, and noticeable in the dry season after it has taken its characteristic woody ball form. Recorded in al-Khashir and Hilifi.

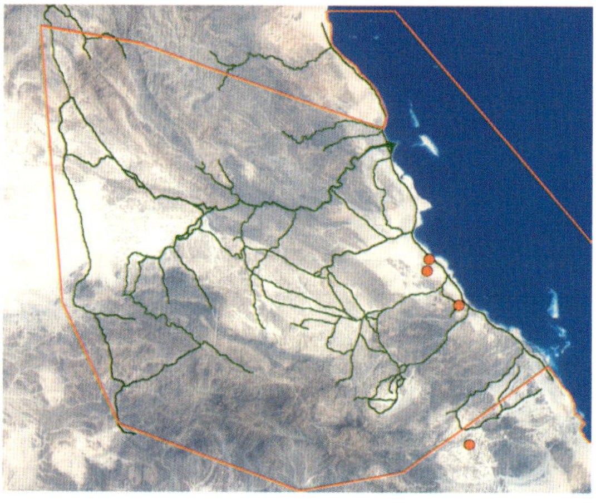

Arnebia hispidissima

(Lehm.) DC., 1846 (Boraginaceae)

Common English name: Prophet Flower

Common local name: (Atan) أتان

Description: An annual herb covered with bristles. Flowers bright yellow, funnel-shaped and arranged in terminal clusters. The roots contain a purplish dye.

Importance and uses: Considered locally as a grazing plant only. In Pakistan a root extract in mustard oil is applied for skin and hair ailments. In India it has been discovered to have anti-cancer properties.

Ecology and distribution: Grows very well in areas of open sand and gravel, especially in years of abundant rainfall. Common in al-Khashir, Umm al-'Abas, and al-Ri'da.

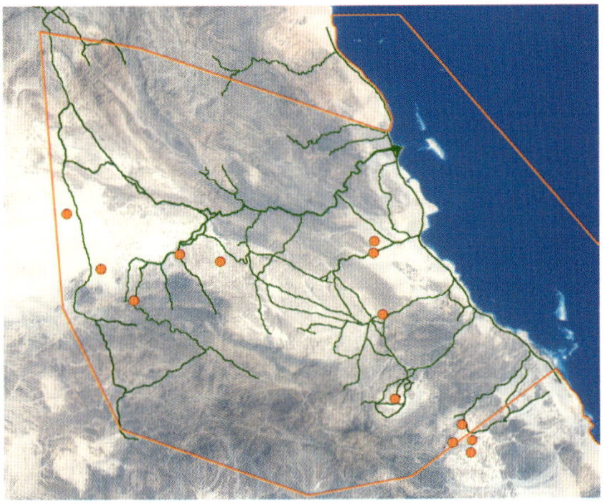

Artemisia judaica

L., 1771(Compositae)

Common English name: Wormwood
Common local name: (Shih) شيح
Description: A perennial herb up to 70 cm high. Stem erect, much-branched. Light green in color, rough, flexible. Aromatic perfume and bitter, persistent taste. Leaves alternate, sessile, simple, variously lobed, and ovate; grayish-green, with smooth velvet touch. Flowers in late spring, with pale yellow flowers.
Importance and uses: The part that grows above ground is cut and collected during the flowering season. An infusion is then used as an antihelminthic, expectorant, diaphoretic, analgesic, and antispasmodic in cases of intestinal colic. Snakes are believed to be repelled by the smoke of burnt branches or by hanging some parts of the plant indoors.
Ecology and distribution: Very rare in the Park. Recorded only in rocky habitats as at Hulus and Hangaliya.

Arthrocnemum macrostachyum

(Moric.) Koch, 1853 (Chenopodiaceae)

Common local name: (Shunan) شنان

Description: A monoecious, perennial halophyte. An almost erect shrub up to 1 m high. Stem appears to be articulated, is glaucous, becoming yellowish-green or reddish. Cymes protrude free then fall to leave a hollow in the segment. Flowers extend to not more than one-third of the length of the segment. Seeds black, with hard coat covered in small knob-like projections. Similar to *Sarcocornia fruticosa*, but with sterile branches that soon become longer than the fertile ones. Prevails on moist salty soils.

Importance and uses: No economic or grazing value. As a primary colonizer of salt pans, it plays an essential role in the succession of salt pans.

Ecology and distribution: Recorded on the coasts of Umm al-'Abas, Hamata region, and Hankurab.

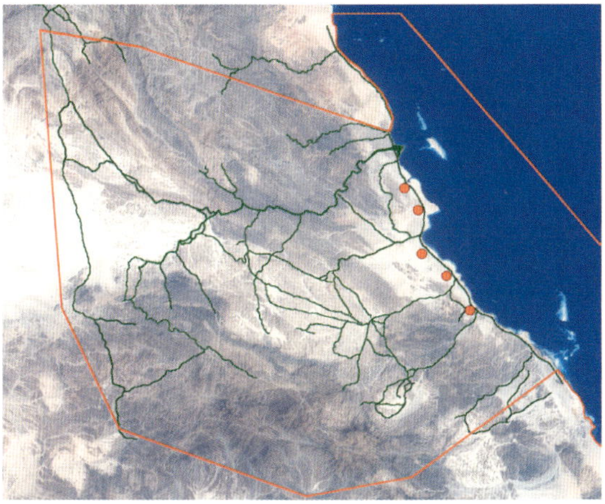

Asphodelus tenuifolius

Cav., 1801 (Liliaceae)

Common English name: Asphodel
Common local name: (Barwag) بروق
The name is derived from composite Greek words (*a* = non-; *spodos* = ashes; *edos* = valley), meaning a valley of the remains not destroyed by fire.
Description: An annual herb with fibrous roots. Seen as a rosette of long basal linear leaves. Scape (the leafless flowering stem) is terete, branched and hollow, with alternate flowers along its length. Flowers with six wax-white, oval tepals each having a central reddish-brown mid-vein. In every scape, the bottom flower opens first, and slowly the flowers above bloom one by one. Seeds black.
Importance and uses: Good grazing plant. The green leaves are eaten locally as fresh vegetables or cooked with *Glossonema boveanum*. In many other regions the seed is used as a diuretic. Also applied externally to ulcers and inflamed parts of the body.
Ecology and distribution: Very common in sandy plains such as al-Ri‘da, Wadi El Gemal, and Abu Ghusun.

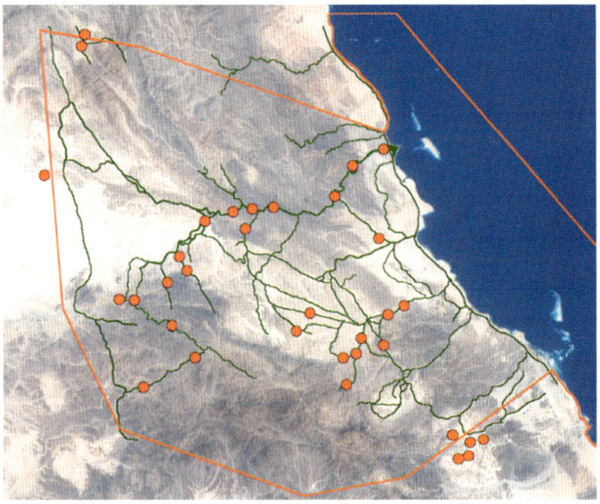

Astragalus eremophilus

Boiss., 1843 (Leguminosa)

Common local name: (Faga'ay) فقعاى

Description: A low, grayish-green, procumbent annual herb. Stems branched from the base, pubescent with both appressed and spreading hairs. Leaves imparipinnately compound with obovate leaflets. Flowers in two to four flowered racemes. Calyx teeth equal or longer than the tube. Corolla pale sulphur yellow. Legume 20–30 mm long, linear, strongly curved, semicircular, grooved, villous, and containing 15–20 seeds.

Importance and uses: A very good grazing plant, with high protein content. No medicinal or traditional use is known locally.

Ecology and distribution: Common in sandy desert. Recorded in Wadi El Gemal, Abu Ghusun, and Kabb al-Khawwara. Flowers February to April.

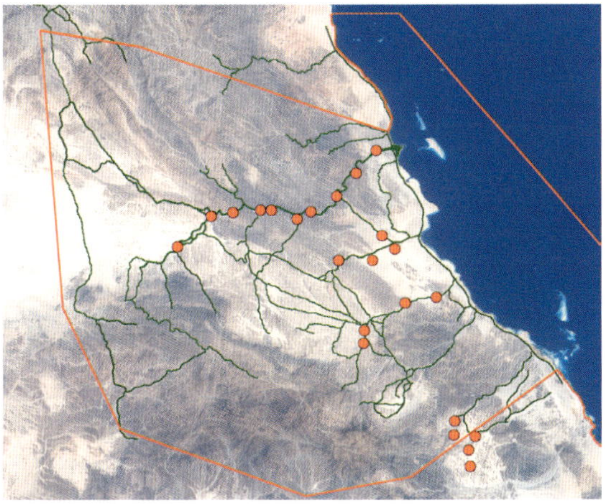

Astragalus vogelii

(Webb) Bornm., 1915 (Leguminosa)

Common local name: (Tawil) تاويل

Description: An annual, white villous herb with a short lifecycle (three to five months) that grows in the desert after rain. Stems prostrate or ascending, and much-branched. Leaves imparipinnate. Flowers pale mauve, included in racemes. Pods oblong-ovoid, turgid,with white appressed hairs.

There are two subspecies in the park:

—subsp. *vogelii*

in which the racemes are compact (right, top two photos).

—subsp. *fatmensis*

in which the racemes are lax (right, bottom two photos).

Importance and uses: Temporary pasture for livestock. High grazing worth confirmed by high protein content. Greatly valued as forage by the Bedouin, who claim it encourages fertility and milk production in their animals.

Ecology and distribution: The two subspecies are common in sandy plains and desert wadis. Recorded in Wadi El Gemal, Hankurab, Abu Ghusun, and Umm al-'Abas.

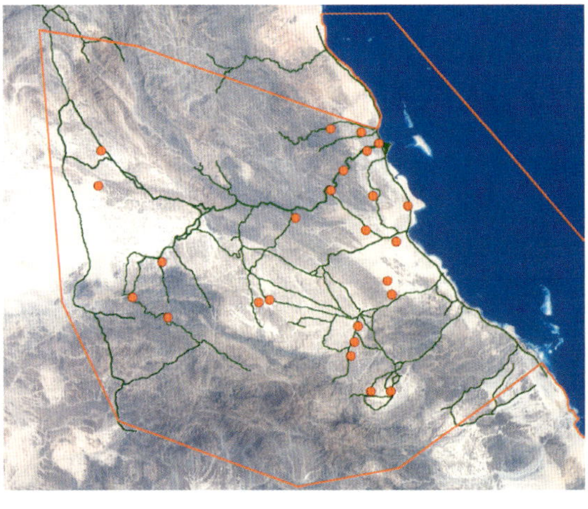

Atriplex farinosa

Forssk., 1775 (Chenopodiaceae)

Common local name: (Handa'al) هندآل

Description: A perennial shrub 0.5 to 1.2 m high, densely mealy all over, whitish-gray. Leaves ovate-elliptic, petiolate, entire, cordate, or auriculate at the base and with obtuse apex. Flowers unisexual, arranged in terminal leafless panicles. Fruits enclosed in large bracteoles.

Importance and uses: No local economic or medicinal value. Ecological importance in accumulating sand, helping plant succession process along the coast. Rarely grazed by animals.

Ecology and distribution: Common in coastal sandy soil, especially in Wadi El Gemal Island, Hankurab, Ras Bughdadi, and Hamata islands.

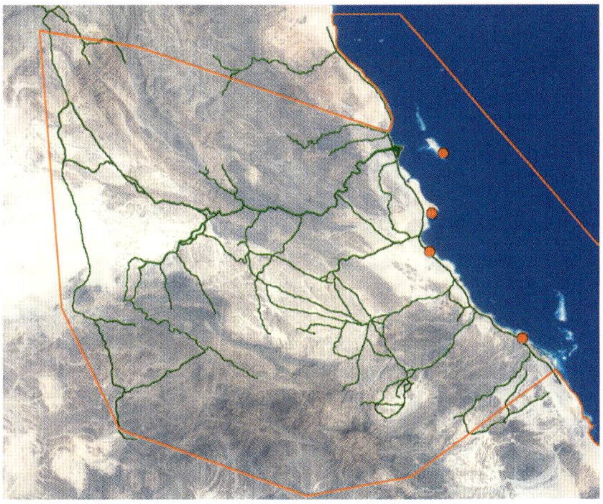

Avicennia marina

(Forssk.) Vierh., 1907 (Aviceniaceae)

Common English name: Gray mangrove
Common local name: (Shura) شورى , (Manjaruf) مَنجَرُوفْ
Description: An evergreen perennial plant. Bark gray and lightly fissured. Extensive root system: many respiratory roots (pneumatophores), covered with lenticels. Leaves opposite, ovate with an acute apex, glossy green above, the lower surface covered with white tomentose. Salt is secreted from the lower surface. Flowers orange. Fruits usually singles and compressed.
Importance and uses: Much is written about its importance. In summary, mangrove swamps serve as valuable nursery areas for several species of fish and invertebrates. They also provide the sea with large amounts of essential dissolved organic carbon. They protect shorelines from erosion and offer nesting and resting areas for birds. Locals use them as forage for camels. Honey is collected from bees that feed on mangrove flower nectar.
Ecology and distribution: Grows in the intertidal zone on the shores of estuaries. One of the few green plants that can survive with their roots in salt water and leaves in the air. Recorded at 9 sites, but mostly in Hamata, Wadi El Gemal Island, and Hirtway.

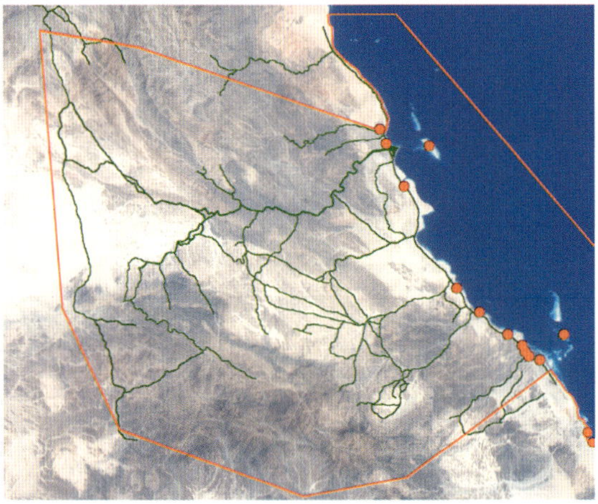

Balanites aegyptiaca

(L.) Delile, 1814 (Balanitaceae)

Common English name: Desert date, Egyptian balsam
Common local name: (Higlig) هجليج, (Lalub) لالوبْ, (Balah al-sukkar) بلح السكر
Description: One of the most common but neglected wild plant species of the drylands. An evergreen spiny tree up to 8 m high. Young stems and spines are grayish-green, becoming light brown. Leaves often glabrescent, subsessile, or with a petiole and leathery. Flowers on spineless branches and yellowish or blue-green. Fruit is date-like, elongating in early stages, becoming ovoid and yellow at ripening.
Importance and uses: Known for its many uses, such as grazing, fuel wood, timber, and so on. The wood is hard, durable, and worked easily; and is used for wooden spoons, pestles, mortars, handles and camel saddles. Fruit is edible; main local use of fruits as antidiabetic. Studies have revealed additional uses such as pesticide and antihelminthic. Active compounds are saponins. In some regions, seeds are crushed to produce cooking oil.
Ecology and distribution: Common in sandy and stony soils. Wadi El Gemal is characterized by rich stands of *B. aegyptiaca*. Common also in Durunkat, Hafafit.

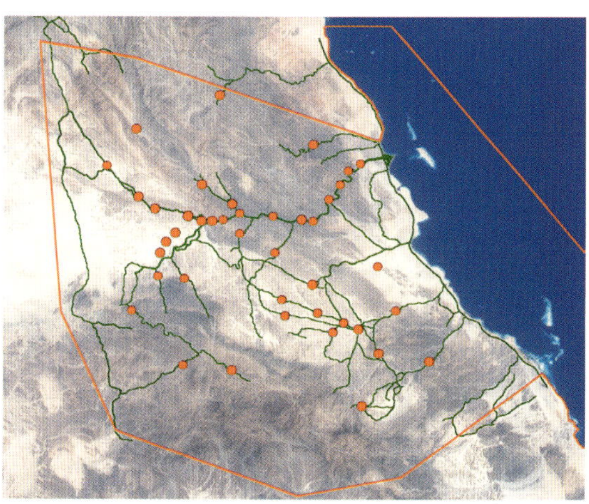

Blepharis edulis

Frossk., 1806 (Acanthaceae)

Common local name: (Khashir) خشير

Description: A spiny, short-lived, perennial herb. Stem rigid, four leaves in each node; leaves and bracts rigid, of silvery appearance and recurved, spiny-tipped and prickly-toothed. Flowers blue in a dense bracteate spike inflorescence. Seeds enclosed in capsules, two seeds in each.

Importance and uses: Charcoal from roots is ground into a powder as an eye powder (kohl) for feeble sight, probably anti-cataract. Seeds considered aphrodisiac and diuretic.

Ecology and distribution: A rare plant. Recorded mainly in stony habitats such as al-Khashir, Umm 'Abd al-Gid, and Hakrahub.

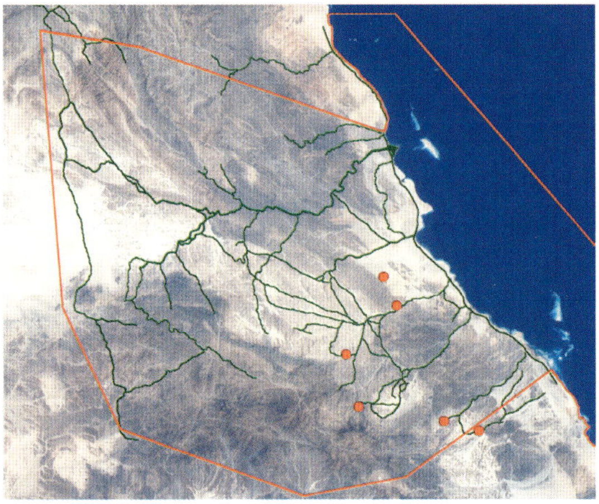

Calligonum polygonoides subsp. *comosum*

L., 1753 (Polygonaceae)

Common local name: (Arta) ارطى

Description: A perennial shrub with much-branched stem. Grows up to 1.2 meters high. The main branch woody, rigid, and covered with soft whitish bark. Young branches look like wisps from a broom. Leaves small subulate and soon deciduous; one may think it leafless.

Importance and uses: Good fodder for cattle and important habitat element for a number of species of semi-desert wildlife. In India the flowers are used to prepare Rayat which is a traditional Indian salad. In Pakistan, the aerial parts are burnt to create a smoke ring to act as fly repellant. No local medicinal importance.

Ecology and distribution: Grows on deep sandy formations with low to medium salinity levels. Very rare in the Park. Recorded only in Hankurab.

Calotropis procera

(Aiton) Aiton, 1811 (Asclepiadaceae)

Common English name: Sodom's milkweed, Sodom apple, mudar, rooster tree, rubber bush, small crown flower

Common local name: ('Ushar) عشار

Description: A spreading shrub or small tree up to 4 m, exuding copious milky sap when cut or broken. Leaves opposite, gray-green and large: up to 15 cm long and 10 cm broad. Flowers waxy-white and purple-tipped inside. Fruits gray-green, inflated, containing numerous seeds with tufts of long silky hairs at one end.

Importance and uses: Bedouin use the powder of the burned leaves in treating skin blisters and abscesses. However, accidental exposure to the latex causes serious congestion of the eyes and may lead to blindness. In other regions used for other purposes: a decoction is used in veterinary medicine; powdered dried leaves are vermifuge in small doses.

Ecology and distribution: Grows in fine sandy soils. Usually as secondary vegetation after the eradication of Acacia trees for fuel. Recorded in Wadi El Gemal, Hafafit, and Hulus.

Capparis decidua

(Forssk.) Edgew., 1862 (Capparacea)

Common local name: (Tundub) طندب

Description: A spinous, bushy shrub or small tree. Usually leafless or very small leaves with short life span on young shoots. Small, light brown spines occur in pairs on the twigs at each node. Flowers pink, helmet-shaped. Fruits are small pink berries of the size and shape of a cherry, becoming blackish when dry.

Importance and uses: The fruits are tasty are eaten by people. Flowers and buds edible. Small branches used to make good-quality prayer beads and hair combs. In other regions, top shoots and young leaves used as plasters for boils and swellings. Consumption of the fruit is said to enhance memory; it is an anthelmintic, analgesic, and aphrodisiac. The bark extract is used for the treatment of asthma and coughs.

Ecology and distribution: Grows in sandy and gravelly soils, thriving on shallow, hard soils and rocky habitats. Recorded in Wadi El Gemal, al-Ludayyid, and Abu Ghusun.

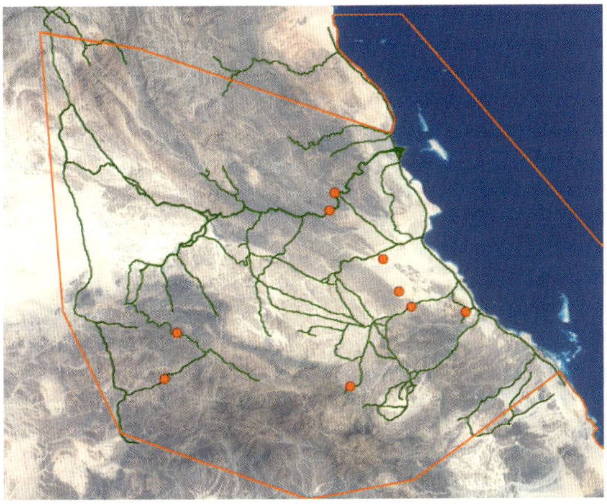

Capparis spinosa

L., 1753 (Capparacea)

Common English name: Caper, caperbush

Common local name: (Lasaf) لصف

Description: A shrubby perennial plant up to 80–150 cm high, with numerous branches. Has a pair of hooked spines at the base of each leaf stalk. Leaves alternate, round to ovate, thick, and glistening. Flowers about 5 cm in diameter, white with numerous pinkish stamens. Produces large green fruits turning to shiny red when ripe. Seeds gray-brown, large, kidney-shaped.

Importance and uses: In addition to the grazing value of caper, the red and green fruit is used for pickles, while the red fruit is eaten fresh. The fruits are dried and ground locally as a decoction for catarrh. Root extract is used to treat rheumatism and paralysis.

Ecology and distribution: Grows well in cracks; found mainly on large rocks or small hills as in Wadi El Gemal and Abu Ghusun. May also appears in sandy plains such as ‘Iri‘ar.

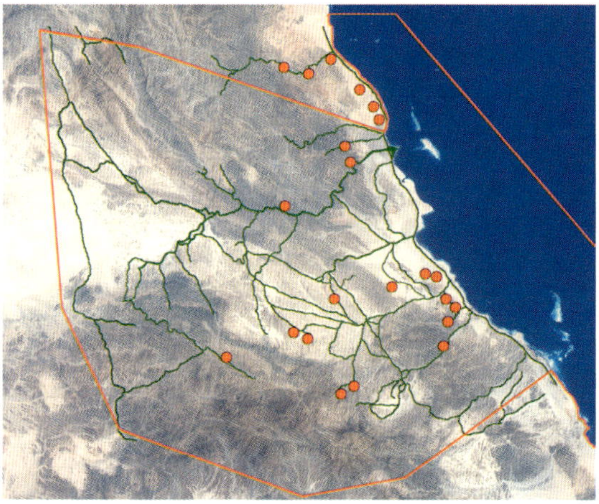

Caylusea hexagyna

(Frossk.) (1929) (Resedaceae)

Common local name: (Danaban) دنبان

Description: A papilose, hairy annual herb up to 15–50 cm high. Stem erect or with long, procumbent, slender branches spreading along the ground. Leaves subsessile, linear-lanceolate, acuminate and the margins undulate. Racemes spike-like, dense, and bracteate. Bracts minute and usually deciduous. Pedicels 1–3 mm. Petals white and longer than sepals. Carpels almost free, two-seeded.

Importance and uses: Grazing. No other local value.

Ecology and distribution: Grows in sandy and stony desert and plains. Recorded in Wadi El Gemal, al-Ludayyid, and Abu Ghusun.

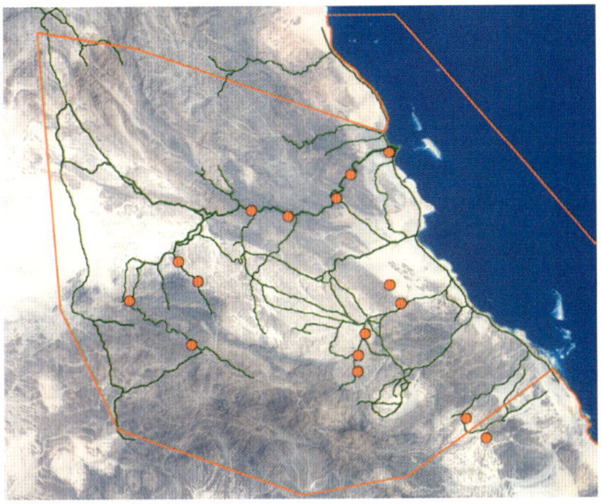

Chenopodium murale

L., 1753 (Chenopodiaceae)

Common English name: Nettleleaf goosefoot
Common local name: (Lisan al-tayr) لسان الطير
Description: An annual herb. Stem generally branched and angular. Leaves fairly thick and usually shiny green on upper surface. Lower leaves opposite, upper alternate. Young leaves have a moist, dewy coating on the lower surfaces, with a strong scent when crushed. Leaves have unequal teeth on the margin. Mature plants up to 90 cm high,with branches arising mostly from the base of the main stem. Flowers greenish, small, in lax raceme and at the tips of the main stem and branches. Good growth when shaded by big trees (right, top), individuals exposed to direct sun have purplish stem (right, center).
Importance and uses: Grazing. No other local use.
Ecology and distribution: Grows well in sandy soil. Common in Wadi El Gemal, al-Ri'da, and Abu Ghusun.

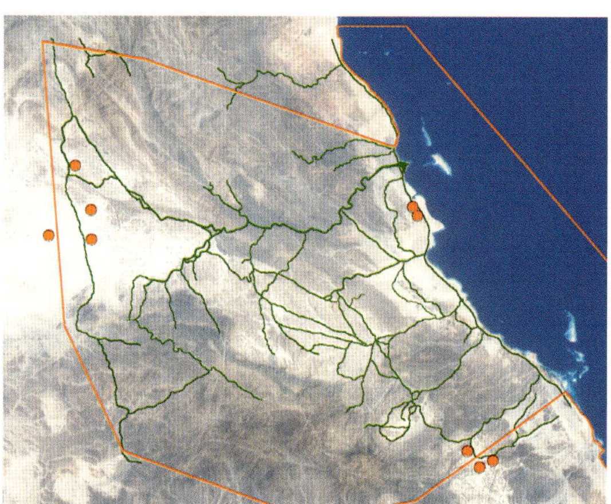

Chrozophora tinctoria

(L.) Raf., 1813 (Euphorbiaceae)

Common English name: *tinctoria* (Latin) = indicates a plant used in dyeing or with a sap that can stain.

Common local name: (Nila) نيلة

Description: An ash-gray-green herb or undershrub. Covered with white, wool-like stellate hairs. Mature leaves have a long petiole and a rhombic to ovate shape. Monoecious. Male flowers above the basal female flowers in the spike-like raceme. Fruit is a capsule with the shape of three spherical bodies fused in a rather rounded-triangular structure. Each fruit holds three seeds. On reaching full maturity, it eventually bursts open with an incredible strong sudden twist of its walls, ejecting the seeds to a considerable distance.

Importance and uses: Locally only a grazing plant, but reported to have medicinal properties as an emetic, cathartic, and fever eliminator. It also produces an indigo dye used for dyeing linen.

Ecology and distribution: Common in sandy plains like in Wadi al-Abyad.

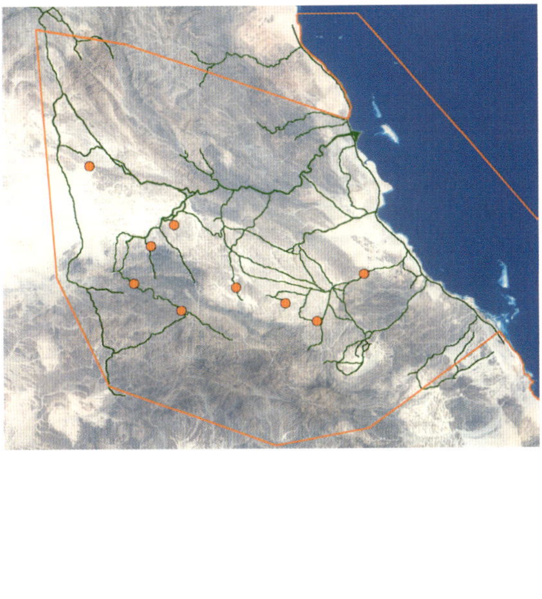

Citrullus colocynthis

(L.) Schrad., 1838 (Cucurbitaceae)

Common English name: Desert squash, Colocynth, Bitter apple

Common local name: (Handal) حنضل

Description: A perennial, scabrous herbaceous trailing plant. Rough angular stems. Leaves also rough, and lobed. Monoecious, with yellow male and female flowers. Fruits are nearly globular, about the size of a small orange, green, and yellow variegated, becoming yellow when ripe, with hard rind, spongy pulp, and intensely bitter.

Importance and uses: One of the most famous medicinal plants. The leaves are diuretic and the roots are useful for rheumatism, joint pains, and externally for ophthalmia. The fruit is cooling, purgative, and carminative, curing ulcers, asthma, and throat diseases. The fruit pulp is purgative, diuretic, and antiepileptic; the hot sap of the plant is used to cure camel skin diseases. In addition to its medicinal value, it is very palatable to gazelles.

Ecology and distribution: Grows well on the sandy soil, as in Abu Ghusun, Wadi El Gemal, and Hafafit.

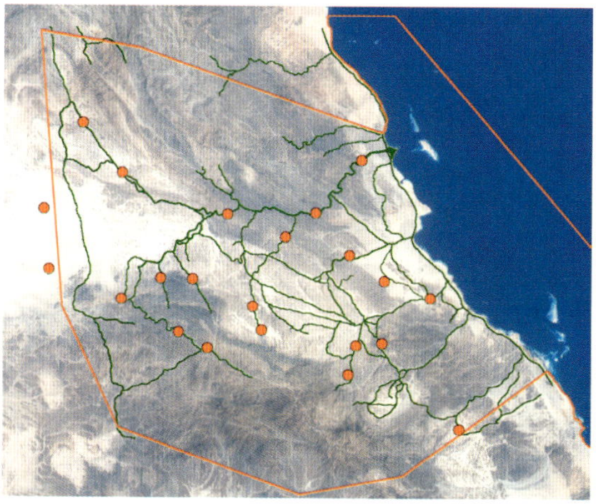

Cleome amblyocarpa

Barratte & Murb., 1905 (Capparacea)
Syn *C. africana*

Common local name: ('Abal al-'ajuz) عبل العجوز
('Uffayn 'atmud) عفين عتمود

Description: An annual glandular-pubescent herb. Foetid, with a disagreeable smell, up to 80 cm high. Stem erect, much-branched, and covered by glandular hairs that trap a layer of dust and small sand particles. Lower leaves are three-foliolate, upper ones simple. Leaflets elliptic. Flowers are pale yellow tipped with reddish-brown and arranged in lax racemes. Fruits are flat and pendulous. Seeds densely lanate at maturity.

Importance and uses: Local people believe that merely touching the plant may cause headache and stomach pain. Active materials, especially Dammarane compounds, are isolated from this plant and acts as an antimicrobial. Used against bacterial infections.

Ecology and distribution: Grows in desert wadis and sandy plains. Recorded in Hafafit and al-Nuhud.

Cleome brachycarpa

DC., 1824 (Capparacea)

Common local name: (Sifirayat al-dan) صفراية الضان

Description: An annual herb or often perennial with a woody base. Viscid, pubescent, mainly erect and branched mostly from the base. Leaves are three–five-foliolate: the lower leaves petiolate, the uppermost simple. Racemes are lax with leafy bracts. Flowers yellow with glandular sepals. Seeds plentiful, brown, and enclosed in a densely glandular oblong capsule.

Importance and uses: Grazing, especially for sheep and goats: hence the local name, Dan.The crushed leaves of it and *Helichrysum* sp. were used as a deodorant for long time in the UAE. In addition to isolation of antimicrobial materials used against bacterial infections. It is an appetite enhancer and carminative.

Ecology and distribution: Rare in the Park. Grows in stony wadis and sandy plains. Recorded in Hankurab and Sharm al-Luli.

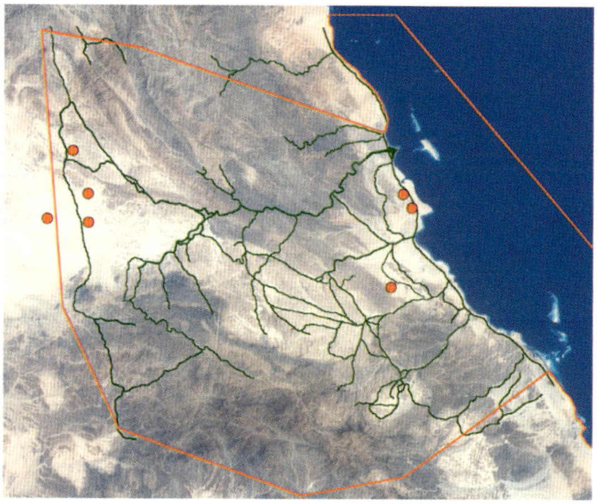

Cleome chrysantha

Decne., 1835 (Capparacea)

Common local name: (Sifiraya) صفراية

Description: A glandular-hairy, perennial herb. Woody at the base, up to 20–50 cm high, stems branched from the base. Branches ascending or procumbent. Leaves simple, ovate, one-nerved, villous, and glandular-hairy and almost acute. Flowers yellow, arranged in the axil of leaf-like bracts in long lax racemes.

Importance and uses: Grazing. No local medicinal value, but recently two active isothiocyanates were isolated from this plant, which exhibit good antimicrobial activity.

Ecology and distribution: Grows in rocky and sandy desert wadis and plains. Recorded in Hafafit, Hulus, Abu Ghusun, and Wadi El Gemal.

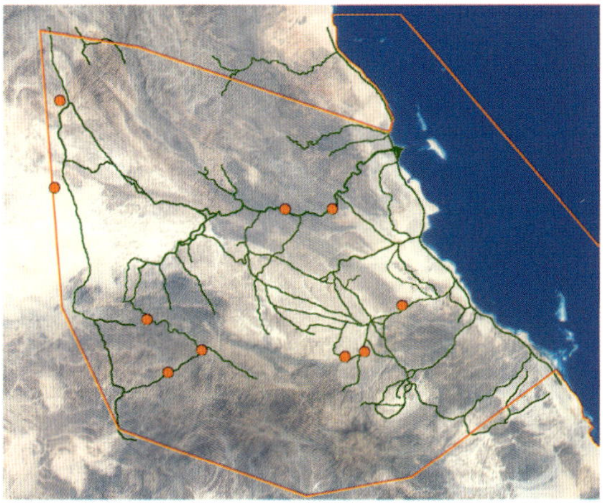

Cleome droserifolia

(Forssk.) Delile, 1814 (Capparacea)

Common local name: ('Uffayn) عفين
Other common names: (Samwa) سموا
Description: A low, perennial, aromatic, and intricate shrub. About 60 cm high, densely covered by glandular hair. Color yellowish-green. Leaves broadly ovate and densely glandular-hairy. A characteristic slightly disagreeable smell and bitter taste. Flowers greenish-yellow.
Importance and uses: The air-dried leaves (known also as *al-Samwa*) are used locally by boiling or soaking to treat kidney pains and hyperglycemia (diabetes). Studies have proved that a powder paste used topically for treatment of wounds and dermatitis, together with aqueous extracts, showed good antimicrobial activity. *Samwa*, *Sanamikki*, and *Halfa barr* are considered the most popular herbs in herbalist shops across Egypt.
Ecology and distribution: Grows in rocky and gravelly habitats. Recorded in Wadi El Gemal, Hafafit, Abu Ghusun, and Hankurab.

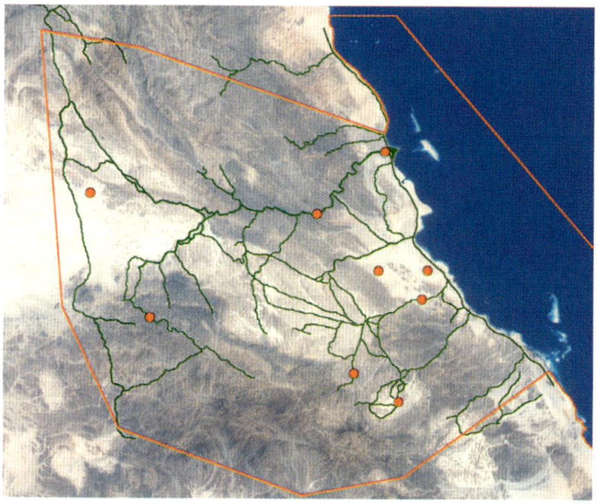

Cocculus pendulus

J. R. and G. Forst., 1910 (Berberidaceae)

Common local name: ('Ullig) عليق

Description: A woody, much-branched shrub. Climbs up cliffs and trees, or may be prostrate. Branches elongate and twining. Leaves leathery, lanceolate-oblong, and glabrous. Small solitary or paired flowers and small, spherical drupe (fruit), shiny red.

Importance and uses: Not recorded as having grazing or medicinal local importance. But some wild animals may graze it, especially in dry seasons.

Ecology and distribution: Recorded in Hilifi, climbing on *Acacia tortilis* trees (right, center). Also recorded in Wadi El Gemal, Abu Ghusun, and Kabb al-Khawwara on some cliffs.

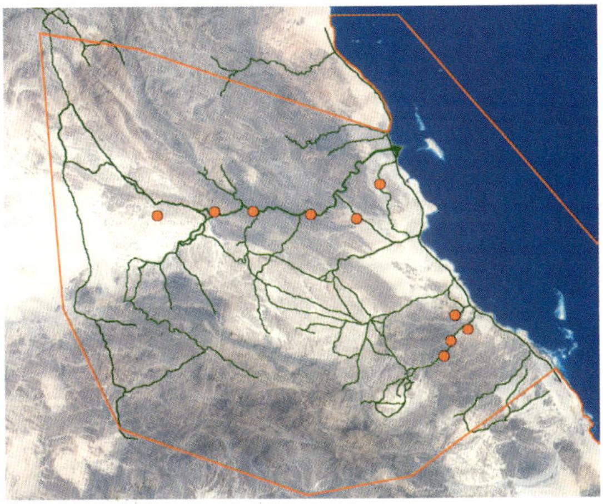

Cometes abyssinica

Wall., 1829 (Cariyophyllaceae)

Common local name: (Dagn al-shaykh) دقن الشيخ

Description: A small, annual, hirsute-scabrous shrub up to 40 cm high. Erect or ascending stem. Leaves linear-lanceolate, occasionally ovate. Bracts to 1.5 cm in fruit. Flowers in three-flowered clusters with oblong and papillose sepals. Petals white. Fruiting heads 1.2 cm in diameter.

Importance and uses: Grazing. Not known to have local medicinal or economic value.

Ecology and distribution: Grows between rocks in stony wadis. Not common in the Park. Recorded in Wadi El Gemal, Abu Ghusun, Hulus, and Hangaliya.

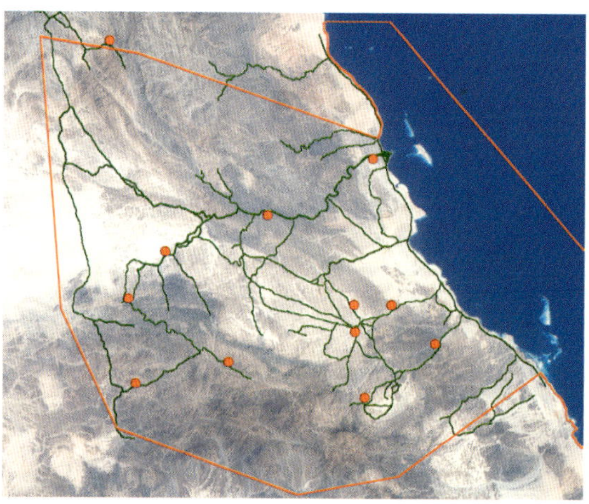

Commicarpus helenae

(Schult.) Meikle, 1971 (Nyctaginaceae)

Common local name: (Hummad al-jabal) حماض الجبل

Other common names: (Widinat al-far) ودينات الفار

Description: A perennial herb from a woody rootstock. Stems up to 1–1.5 m long, slender, erect, decumbent or scrambling, branching, and pubescent or glabrous. Leaves cordate, more or less fleshy glabrous. Flowers in whorls, pink or mauve.

Importance and uses: No known medicinal value. Not good for grazing.

Ecology and distribution: Grows in dry sandy or rocky areas and on calcareous soils. Rare in the Park. Recorded only in al-Ri‘da.

Convolvulus hystrix

Vahl, 1790 (Convolvulaceae)

Common local name: (Shibrig) شبرق

Other common names: (Gurdum) قرضم

Description: A perennial, dark green shrub. Mainly prostrate and densely villous. Stems much-branched; branches strongly entangled with strong spines. Leaves have acute apex and truncate base. Flowers blue, sessile, in dense clusters and with hairy bands on the lower surface.

Importance and uses: Eaten by animals, but no local medicinal or economic value. In other regions, the root is used as a purgative. Recently, scientists isolated useful chemical substances from it, such as vanillin syringic acid.

Ecology and distribution: Rare in the Park. Recorded only on its northern coastal plain. Suffers from overgrazing by goats and camels.

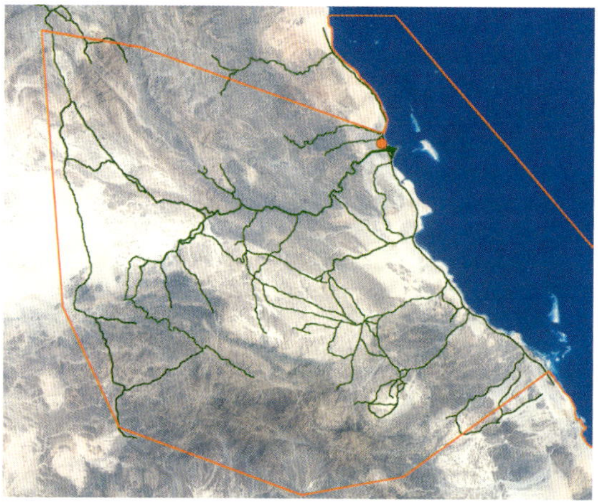

Cornulaca monacantha

Delile, 1814 (Chenopodiaceae)

Common local name: (Shuk al-dib) شوك الديب , (Had) حاد
Description: An intricately branched woody shrub up to 60 cm. Greenish, turning yellowish or whitish when dried, glabrous-glaucous, except the leaf axils. The old stems have cracked bark. Leaves triangular with broad, rounded bases. Flowers in axillary clusters, surrounded by white, woolly hairs; seeds rounded, compressed, and yellowish.
Importance and uses: No local economic or medicinal value. In Morocco a decoction of the leaves is taken on an empty stomach for liver problems and jaundice and as purgative. It is considered excellent pasture for camels, despite the spines on the leaves; it also has a beneficial purgative effect for camels, as well as helping milk production. It is also used as a remedy for scabies.
Ecology and distribution: Grows in sandy plains and desert wadis. Not common in the Park. Recorded in Hankurab region.

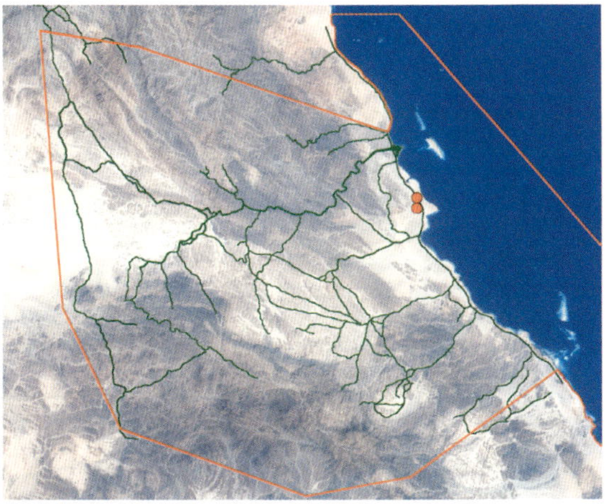

Cotula cinerea

Delile, 1814 (Compositae)

Common local name: (Aribyan) اربيان

Description: A small, gray, woolly erect or ascending annual herb with yellow discoid heads of hemispherical shape. Stems many from the base. Leaves more or less fine-dissected with flat entire lobes, the uppermost leaves smaller, undivided.

Importance and uses: Grazing. In some regions the aromatic infusion of flower heads is used. Useful against vomiting, nausea, scorpion bites, and stomach pains. Ethyl ether extract is highly effective against pathogenic bacteria.

Ecology and distribution: Grows in sandy habitats. Recorded in Wadi El Gemal, Hafafit, Wadi al-Abyad, and Abu Ghusun.

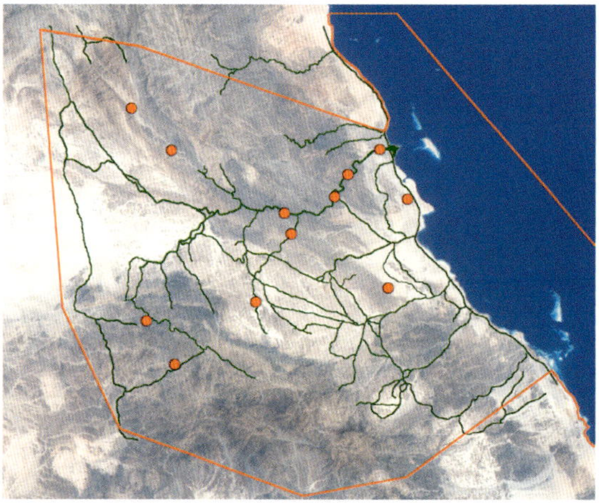

Crotalaria aegyptiaca

Benth., 1843 (Leguminosa)

Common English name: Rattle-box

Common local name: (Natash) نتش

Description: A perennial shrub reaching 60 cm high, and much-branched. Usually leafless at flowering (one of its most obvious features). Stems condensed and ribbed. Old dry plants may revive after rainfall.

Importance and uses: Grazed by camels and gazelles, but poisonous to sheep and goat, so its use as grazing is carefully controlled. Its toxicity is due to the presence of large quantities of hepatotoxic pyrrolizidine alkaloids.

Ecology and distribution: Grows in desert wadis. Rare in the Park. Recorded in Wadi Natash, al-Nuhud region, and Rod 'Abd al-Gid.

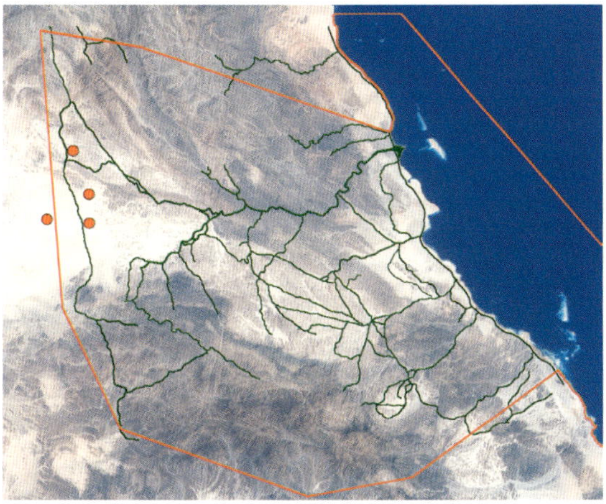

Crotalaria microphylla

Vahl, 1790 (Leguminosa)

Common local name: (Giliglan) قليقلان

Description: An annual herb with prostrate branches up to 70cm long. Many stems from the base, which are slender with stiff, appressed white hairs. Leaves mostly three-foliolate stipulate. Leaflets linear to oblanceolate but stipules linear. Flowers leaf-opposed, pale yellow, sometimes with pale violet veins. Pod oblong-obovoid. About 20–30 seeds per pod and triangular.

Importance and uses: Grazing. Preferred for its high protein content. No local medicinal value.

Ecology and distribution: Grows in sandy plains and gravelly soil. Recorded in al-Ludayyid, Hilifi, al-Riʿda, and al-Khashir.

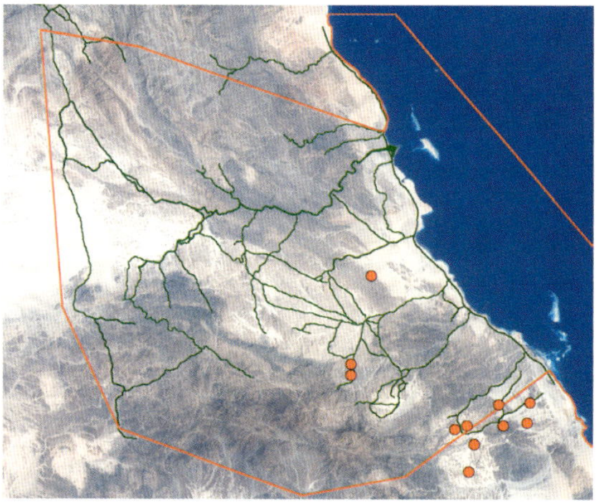

Cucumis prophetarum

L., 1755 (Cucurbitaceae)

Common English name: Globe cucumber
Common local name: (Hinidlan) حنضلان
Description: A perennial plant with woody rootstock, stems trailing to 1.5 meters. Stems light green, grooved, and diverging at the joints. Stiffly hairy and, like *C. colocynthis,* sprouting tendrils at the base of the leaf stalks. Leaves palmate lobed, distinctly veined, crisped at the margins. Flowers often more orange than *C. colocynthis*. A major distinguishing feature is the fruit: this is plum-sized, covered with blunt, spine-like tubercles, striped longitudinally green and yellow, maturing to a very bright yellow.
Importance and uses: In addition to its grazing value, the unripe fruits are pickled like those of its relative, the common cucumber *(Cucumis sativus)*.
Ecology and distribution: Grows in sandy plains. Rare in the Park. Recorded in Hilifi, Wadi El Gemal, and Kabb al-Khawwara

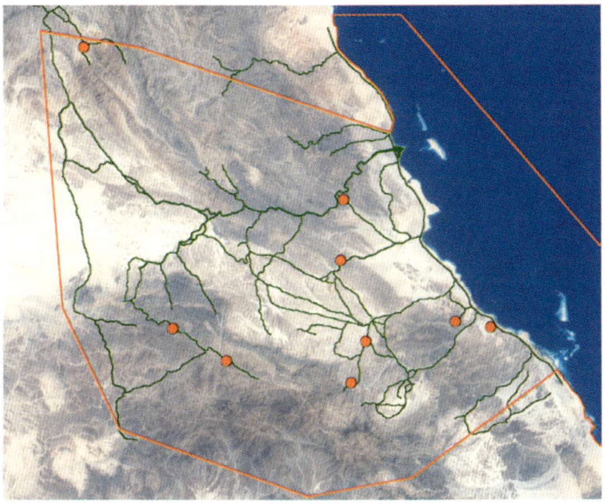

Cuscuta sp.

Lam., 1786 (Convolvulaceae)

Common English name: Dodders, Goldthread, Hairweed

Common local name: (Hamul) حامول

Description: A leafless, annual plant with hair-like branching stems. Parasitic, without chlorophyll, developing penetrating suckers. Considered a destructive weed.

Importance and uses: No local use. In China, the seeds are used with other herbs to treat a wide range of conditions, from impotence, premature ejaculation, and frequent urination to blurred vision and dry eyes.

Ecology and distribution: Recorded only once, in Hulus, covering *Lycium shawii*, causing great harm by penetrating the stem, branches, and even leaves.

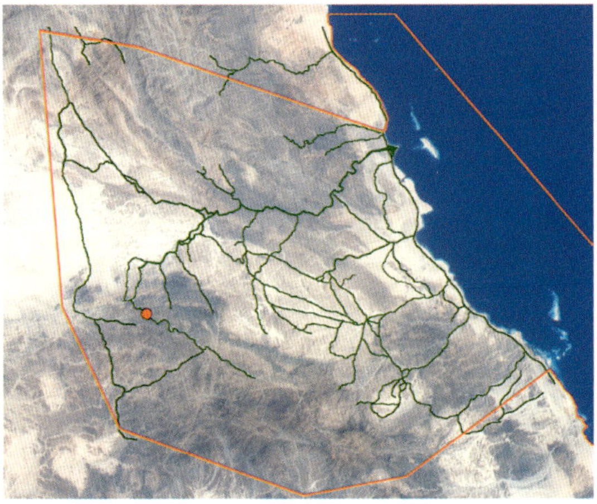

Cyperus conglomeratus
Rottb., 1772 (Cyperaceae)

Common English name: Sedge
Common local name: ('Ishub) عشوب
Description: A yellowish-green perennial, at intervals tufted. Roots long, thick, and covered with sand-binding hairs. Rhizomes short and branched, or elongate, covered by acute purple-brown scales. Spikes broadly ovate to spherical, digitate clusters of brown spikelets.
Importance and uses: Grazing in the absence of other plants. In other regions it is used as pectoral, emollient, diuretic, stimulant, analgesic and anthelmintic treatment (Boulos, 1983).
Ecology and distribution: Grows inland and on coastal sand dunes and desert sandy plains. Drought-resistant, widely distributed. Recorded along the coastal plain, in Hankurab and Wadi El Gemal, also inland, in Hafafit. (Right, top: during the dry season. Right, center and bottom: four months after the flood.)

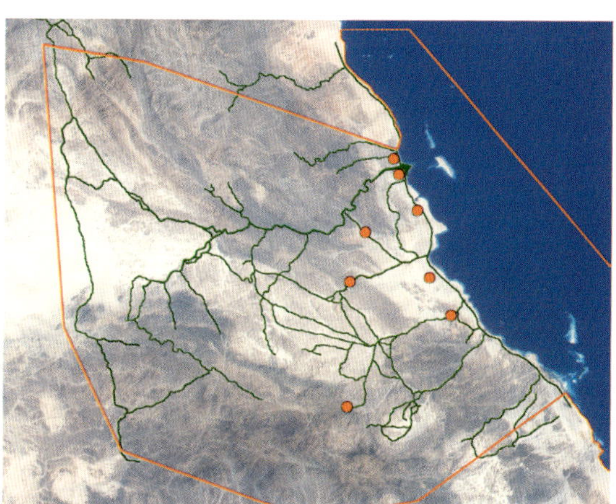

Echinops spinosissimus

L., 1767 (Compositae)

Common English name: Thorny-headed globe thistle
Common local name: (Siha) سحا
Other common names: (Singid) سنقد
Description: A perennial herb. Clumps of deeply divided, spiny leaves, gray-green above, fuzzy-white beneath. Round, compact heads of tiny pale blue or grayish-white flowers, resembling thistles, atop long skinny, gray-white stems in late summer. Despite the flowers' thorny heads, insects and bees are not deterred.
Importance and uses: Grazing. No local medicinal or economic value. In other regions it is highly reputed as a diuretic, nerve tonic, and cough suppressant, and contains a range of sesquiterpene lactones.
Ecology and distribution: All records observe stony habitats or foothills. Recorded in Hulus, Hakrahub, Hangaliya, and Rumit.

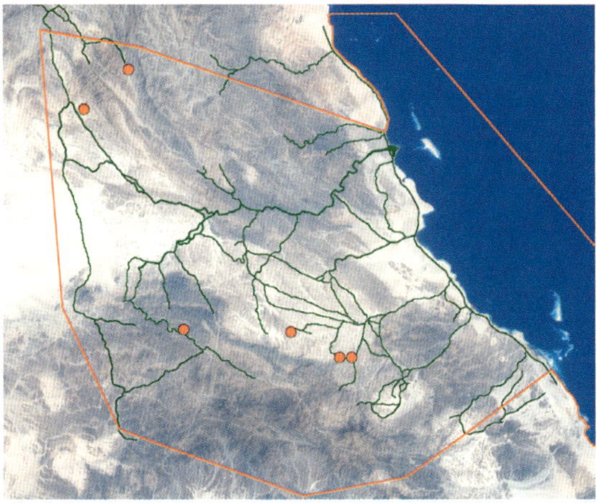

Echium horridum

Batt., 1892 (Boraginaceae)

Common local name: (Kahali) كحالى

Description: A hispid, setose annual or short-lived perennial herb with much-branched stem. Branches angular and erect or ascending. Leaves oblong-lanceolate and petiolate, the upper leaves sessile. Large irregular flowers in terminal cymes. Flowers bracteate, blue or violet, purple when mature. Corolla funnel-shaped, curved with open throat.

Importance and uses: Grazing. No local known medicinal value. It contains echimidine as a major pyrrolizidine alkaloid. Extracts of the aerial parts inhibit the growth of gram-negative bacteria *Escherichia coli* and *Klebsiella* and of the fungus *Candida albicans.*

Ecology and distribution: Grows well in sandy desert plains and stony wadis. Recorded in Hulus, Hangaliya, and Abu Hamamid.

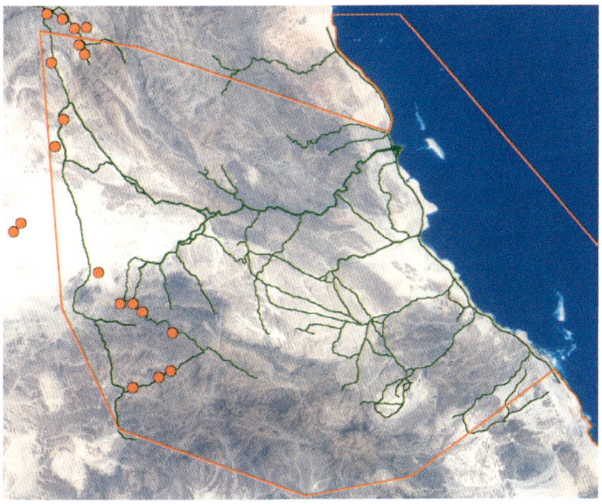

Erodium laciniatum

(Cav.) Willd., 1800 (Boraginaceae)

Common English name: Cut-leaved cranesbill
Common local name: (Kiryayit) كريايت
Other common names: (Gurayn) قرين
Description: A hairy, annual herb. About 15–50 cm high. Stem ascending or procumbent. Leaves mostly pinnatipartite and petiolate. Flowers purple, arranged in umbel-like structures, with three–eight flowers each. Sepals are appressed hairy.
Importance and uses: Modern research proves that *E. laciniatum* acts as a benefactor species to nearby smaller annuals by increasing their performance (i.e., their biomass or survival). Grazing. No other local value.
Ecology and distribution: Grows in sandy plains and desert wadis. Recorded in Hankurab, Wadi El Gemal, Hafafit, and Kabb al-Khawwara.

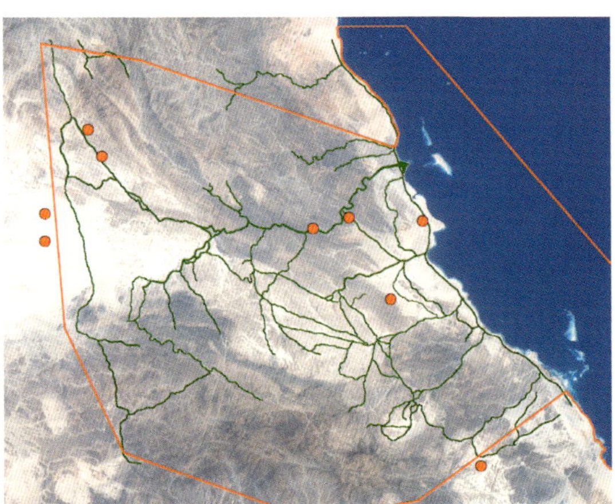

Euphorbia granulata

Forssk., 1775 (Euphorbiaceae)

Common local name: (Lubbayn) لبين

Description: A prostrate annual herb with a short life-cycle (three–five months) that grows in the desert after rain. About 5–25 cm high, covered by short, straight hairs, or sparsely covered by long spreading hairs. Stem much-branched from the base, pale purplish. Leaves small, opposite, petiolate, obovate to oblong-ovate with obliquely rounded base, with rounded apex and entire margin. Upper surface of leaves glabrous. Flowers unisexual.

Importance and uses: Temporary pasture for livestock. No local medicinal value but Touareg people of the Sahara use the latex internally to expel intestinal worms, and externally apply it to snake-bites and scorpion sting. In Saudi Arabia the latex is taken as a purgative, anthelmentic, and diuretic.

Ecology and distribution: Grows in sandy plains. Recorded in Wadi El Gemal, Abu Ghusun, Hafafit, and al-Khashir.

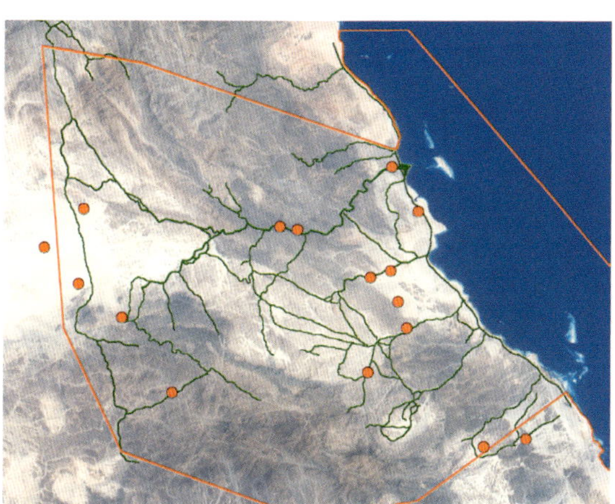

Fagonia mollis

Delile, 1814 (Zygophyllaceae)

Common local name: (Kasha'id al-hamir) كشائيد الحمير

Description: A low perennial shrub up to 20–40 cm high, with woody base, hairy, sessile glands. Stem many branched from the base, angular. Leaves opposite, with spiny stipules. Flowers solitary, pedicellate, bisexual and pink. Fruits are capsules deeply five-lobed.

Importance and uses: Grazing. No local medicinal use. In other regions used to treat illnesses and temporary conditions including psychological fears, also to relieve toothache, headache, and even as an antibiotic.

Ecology and distribution: Thrives in many different habitats and under different conditions. Grows in sandy (right, top) and stony wadis (right, center). Recorded in Abu Ghusun, Wadi El Gemal, and Wadi al-Abyad.

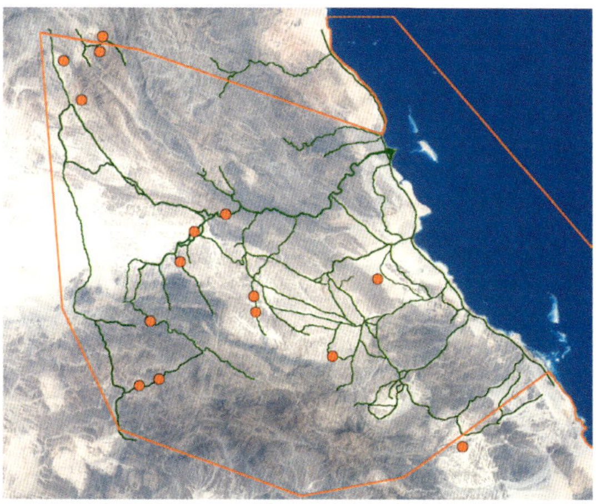

Farsetia longisiliqua

Decne., 1835 (Cruciferae)

Common local name: (Huk) هوك

Description: A perennial herb with woody base. Grows up to 40–80 cm high with richly branched stem. Leaves linear, up to 5 cm long. Flowers in long lax racemes, much elongated in fruiting. Sepals up to 1 cm, petals up to 2 cm, white to pale yellow. The siliqua (fruits) are up to 4.5 cm, with six seeds per siliqua.

Importance and uses: Grazing. No other local medicinal or economic value.

Ecology and distribution: Grows well in stony wadis and slopes, rarely in sandy plains. Recorded in Umm ‘Abd al-Gid, Wadi El Gemal, and Abu Ghusun.

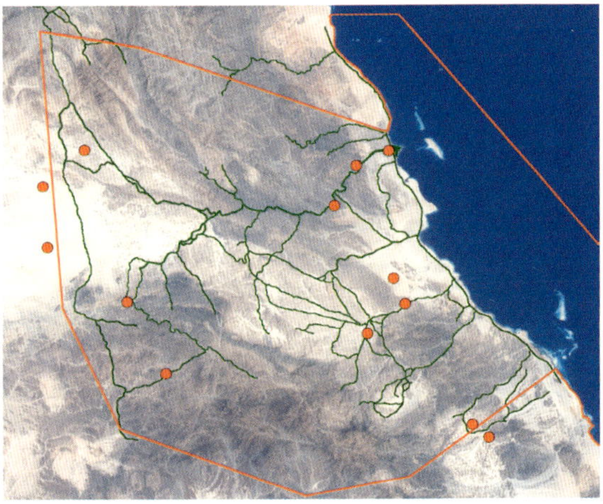

Farsetia stylosa

R.Br., 1826 (Cruciferae)

Common local name: (Huk ‘atmud) هوك عتمود

Description: Annual or short-lived herb. Grows up to 20–60 cm high, sometimes with woody base. Stems much-branched, ascending. Leaves up to 8 cm, linear to linear-elliptic. Flowers white to mauve, in lax racemes which are much elongatd in fruiting. Sepals, petals, and siliqua shorter than in *F. longisiliqua.* One to two seeds per siliqua.

Importance and uses: Grazing. No other local value.

Ecology and distribution: Rare in the Park. Recorded in stony wadis and slopes such as Umm ‘Abd al-Gid and Wadi El Gemal.

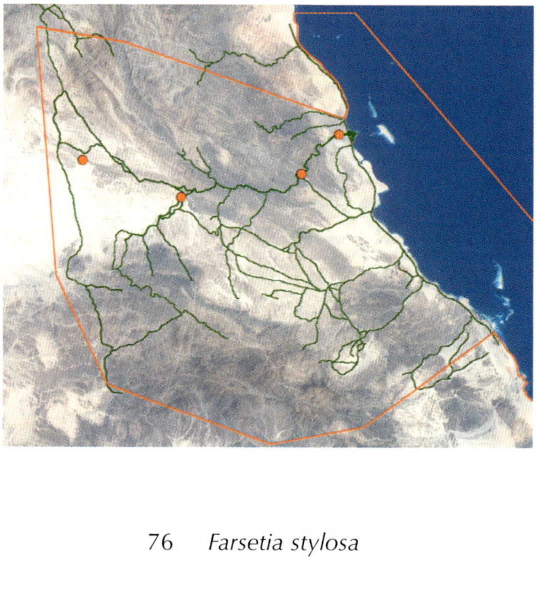

Ficus palmata

Forssk., 1775 (Moraceae)

Common English name: Wild fig

Common local name: (Hummat) حماط

Other common names: (Tin Barri) تين برى (Samyuk) سميوك

Description: Called Hummat in Arabic. The name 'Hamata mountains' comes from the plant, which is common there. A deciduous moderate-sized tree, 6–10 m high. Young branches tomentose, often becoming glabrous. Leaves alternate, broad, ovate, with dentate margin; dark green and rough on the upper surface, light green and tomentose on the lower surface. Flowers unisexual. Fig (fruit) develops from the hollow, globose, fleshy receptacle. Seeds numerous, round, and very small.

Importance and uses: A delicious fruit, much enjoyed. In India, the fruit is also used as demulcent, emollient, laxative, and poultice, and as part of the diet for constipation and diseases of the lungs and bladder. The sap is used for warts.

Ecology and distribution: Grows in rocky cliffs and wadi sides. Not common in the Park. Recorded only at high altitudes such as in the Sartut hills and Hamata mountains.

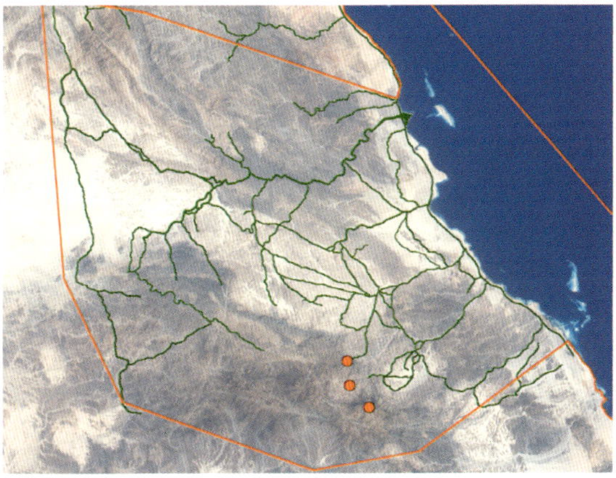

Forsskaolea tenacissima

L., 1764 (Urticaceae)

Common local name: (Lussaq) لصاق

Description: A perennial herb up to 65 cm high, with woody base. Stem erect or ascending, reddish. The whole plant is hispid. Leaves petiolate, stipulate, and ovate-rhombic. Upper side of the leaves with uncinate and straight hairs; the lower side densely white-woolly. Flowers separated into male and female. The ovary surrounded by dense wool.

Importance and uses: Grazing, especially for goats. No local medicinal value; in other regions used as a cure for coughs and headaches.

Ecology and distribution: Grows in rocky wadis, slopes, sandy clay and gravelly soils. Recorded in al-Ludayyid, Abu Hamamid, al-Ri'da, and Hafafit.

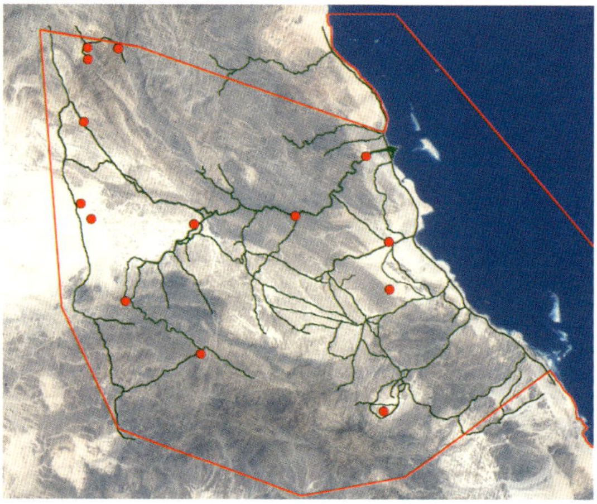

Glossonema boveanum

(Decne.) Decne., (1883). (Asclepiadaceae)

Common local name: (‘Itr) عتر

Description: A hairy, procumbent perennial up to 10–30 cm high. Stem woody and much-branched from the base. Leaves ovate or lanceolate with truncate base and acute apex, the margin usually undulate. Two to six flowers in sessile cymes, with hairy calyx and whitish-yellow, glabrous corolla. Follicle (fruit) ovoid, up to 5 cm long, acuminate pubescent, echinate, greenish. The ripe fruits release small, brownish seeds on long, silky hairs.

Importance and uses: The most delicious fruit in the desert. Also cooked as a vegetable, like okra, and used for grazing. In addition it is found to produce flavonol glycosides. **Ecology and distribution:**

Common in the Park, especially in stony wadis and on mountain slopes. Recorded in Umm ‘Itr, Natash, and Wadi El Gemal.

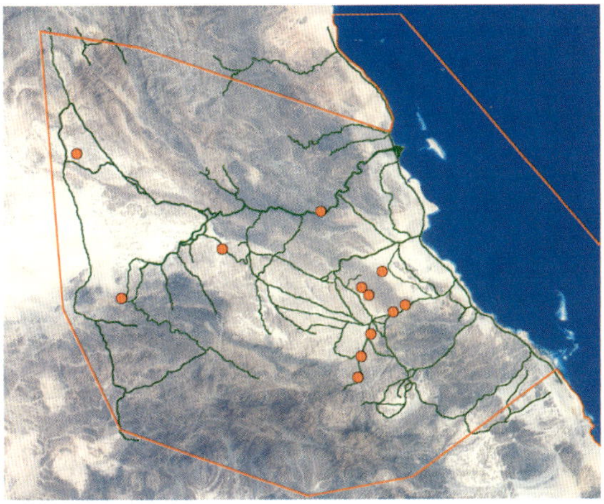

Heliotropium bacciferum

Forssk., 1775 (Boraginaceae)

Common local name: (Rumram) رمرام

Description: A perennial, dark-green herb with woody base and terete stem up to 60 cm high. Pubescent, with white bristles. Many procumbent or ascending branches from the base. Leaves linear- lanceolate, with revolute margin, longer at the base than at the top. Forked terminal inflorescences with small white flowers. Fruits green, nutlet-shaped.

Importance and uses: One of the species preferred by animals. No local medicinal value, although it is said it can be used for snake bites. Used in Cape Verde as a cardiotonic and in North Africa used as repellent for storage insects; in addition some pyrrolizidine alkaloids have been isolated.

Ecology and distribution: Rare in the Park. Recorded in the sandy soil of Hafafit and al-Nuhud.

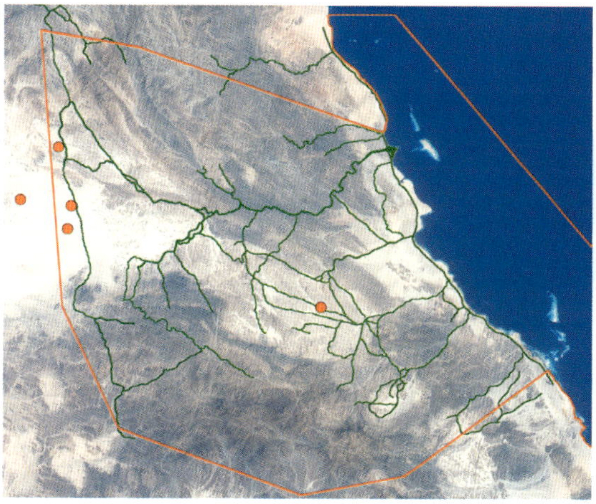

Hippocrepis constricta

Kunze, 1842 (Leguminosa)

Common local name: (Giliglan) قليقلان

Description: A glabrous annual herb up to 10–40 cm high. Prostrate angular stem with many branches from the base with long internodes. The leaf consists of two to five pairs of leaflets. Flowers pale yellow with pink veins, in two to four flowered umbels. Legumes linear, slightly curved with sinuses between seed chamber.

Importance and uses: Good animal pasture because of its high protein content. No local medicinal nor economic value.

Ecology and distribution: Grows in sandy plains and limestone hills. Rare in the Park. Recorded in al-Khashir and al-Ri‘da.

Hyphaene thebaica

(Del.) Mart., 1838–45 (Palmae)

Common English name: Gingerbread tree, Doum-palm
Common local name: (Dom) دوم
Description: A dioecious palm-tree. Trunk fibrous, up to 20 m high, repeatedly bi-forked. Leaves fan-shaped, up to 1 square meter. Fruits in long clusters, each containing between one and 200. Fruits beautifully polished, rich, yellowish-brown, of irregular form up to fist size.
Importance and uses: The edible part of the fruit is the fibrous, mealy husk, which tastes almost exactly like gingerbread. A delicious soft drink is made from this, and molasses are also prepared from the fruit: almost every part of the plant has a use.
Ecology and distribution: Grows mainly in oases, in southern Egypt, and the Red Sea region. Only one batch of male individuals recorded in Wadi El Gemal Delta. This tree is considered a feature of Wadi El Gemal, and we are trying to plant female individuals.

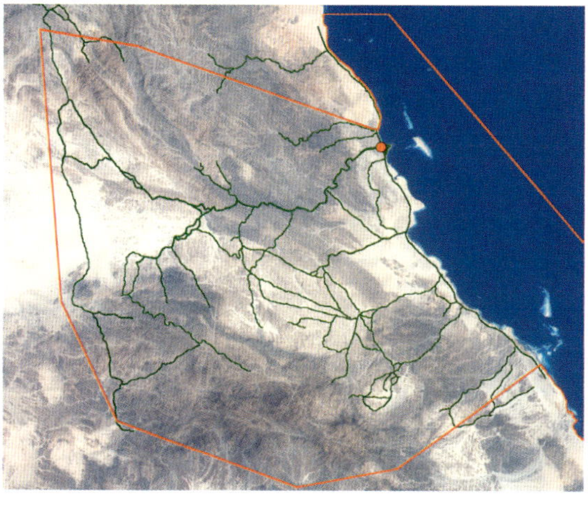

Imperata cylindrica

(L.) Raeusch., 1797 (Gramineae)

Common local name: (Halfa) حلفا

Description: An aggressively rhizomatous perennial grass up to1.2 m high. Forms tufts of leaves from the hard and scaly rhizome, in dense basilar rosette form. Blades flat or loosely enrolled, stiff and erect. Panicles soft, spike-like, cylindrical, obscured by copious silky white hairs from callus and glumes; up to 22 cm long.

Importance and uses: Grazing, epecially in dry seasons. No other local value. In other regions rhizomes used as antipyretic and diuretic. Flowers used in hemoptysis and epistaxis of pulmonary diseases.

Ecology and distribution: Grows in dry or moist sandy places. Recorded in Wadi El Gemal Delta around the brackish water area and in Sartut, around springs.

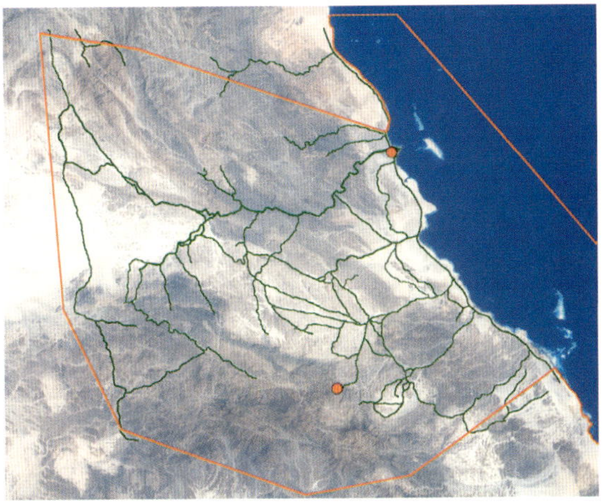

Indigofera spinosa

Forssk., 1775 (Leguminosa)

Common local name: (Shadid) شديد

Description: A spiny, woody dwarf shrub. Indigenous to arid and semi-arid rangelands of northeastern Africa. Stem much-branched, intricate, with appressed white hairs. Rachis very short, with densely strigose leaflets. Flowers red and subsessile on sharp red or yellow needle-like spines.

Importance and uses: Grazing for camels, especially in the absence of better food resources. No other local use. In other regions the root is used for chewing, as a toothache analgesic, and for abdominal disorders.

Ecology and distribution: Rare in the Park. Recorded in al-Ri'da and Abu Ghusun.

Iphiona scabra

DC., 1834 (Compositae)

Common local name: (Bakanun) بكانون

Description: A glandular-hairy, viscid low shrub up to 25–60 cm high. Characteristic scent. Stem densely branched and leaved. Leaves needle-like, rigid, sessile, and acuminate. Flowers yellow, discoid, in rather narrow cup-shaped heads, each with a few flowers. Grows well in desert (right, top) and stony habitats (right, center).

Importance and uses: Grazing; also used for fodder and fuel. No known medicinal use.

Ecology and distribution: Grows in stony and sandy wadis. Recorded in Abu Ghusun, Wadi El Gemal, Hilifi, and Hankurab.

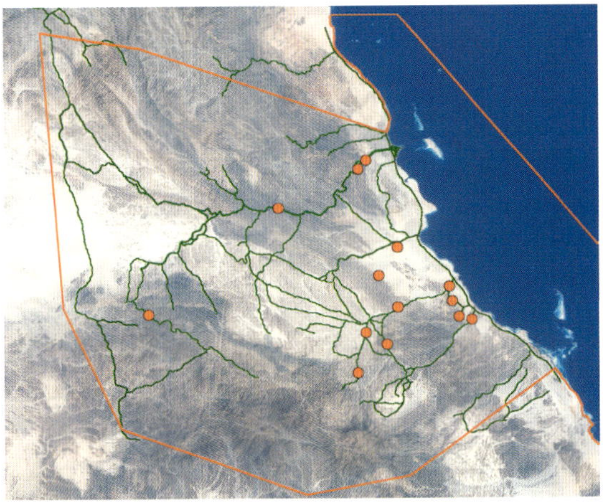

Juncus rigidus

Desf., 1798 (Junicaceae)

Common English name: Hard sea rush
Common local name: (Samar) سمار
Other common names: (Dis) ديس
Description: A salt marsh perennial plant. The *J. rigidus* community forms thickets of dense growth, dominating saline flats in saline-neglected land formerly under cultivation. Represents one of the most common halophytic communities.
Importance and uses: In the Park, considered only a grazing plant. In the Nile delta, used for making traditional mats. Also a source of dyes and oils.
Ecology and distribution: It dominates the brackish parts of the salt marshes. Recorded in two sites across the Park: north of Wadi El Gemal Delta, where soil salinity, organic matter, moisture content and fine material are high; and around water springs in Wadi Sartut.

Kickxia acerbiana

(Boiss.) Taeckh. and Boulos, 1974 (Scrophulariacea)

Common local name: (Widin al-far) ودين الفار

Description: A densely pubescent to somewhat viscid annual or short-lived perennial, up to 50 cm high. Central stem erect, lateral stems ascending. All stems pubescent with both short and long hairs; some hairs glandular. Leaves alternate, short-petiolate, and pubescent like the stem. Leaves greatly reduced upward and becoming acute and densely pubescent. Flowers axillary, solitary along the length of the stem, pale yellow.

Importance and uses: Grazing. No local medicinal or economic value.

Ecology and distribution: Grows in stony wadis, sandy wadis and desert plains. Recorded in Hangaliya, Hulus, Khashir, and Wadi El Gemal.

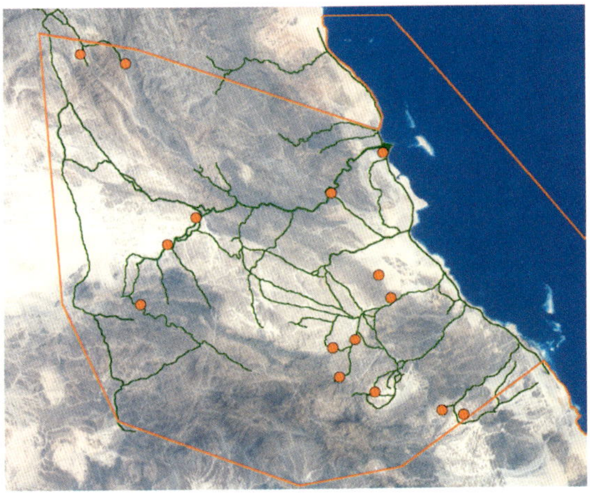

Lavandula coronopifolia

Poir., 1813 (Labiatae)

Common English name: Lavender
Common local name: (Baswi) بسوى
Description: A small shrub up to 1 m high. Angular, rigid, and many-branched stem. Branching is from the base. Pale green. Leaves hairy, deeply lobed. Flowers blue or purple, short pedicellate or subsessile in crowded terminal spikes. Seeds soft and brown.
Importance and uses: Occasional local use to relieve stomach pains. Modern studies prove that it contains many important active materials such as linalol, geraniol, and caryophyllene. Grazing.
Ecology and distribution: Grows in rocky habitats and in foothills. Recorded between rocks in Hulus, Hilifi, al-Ludayyid, and the Hamata hills.

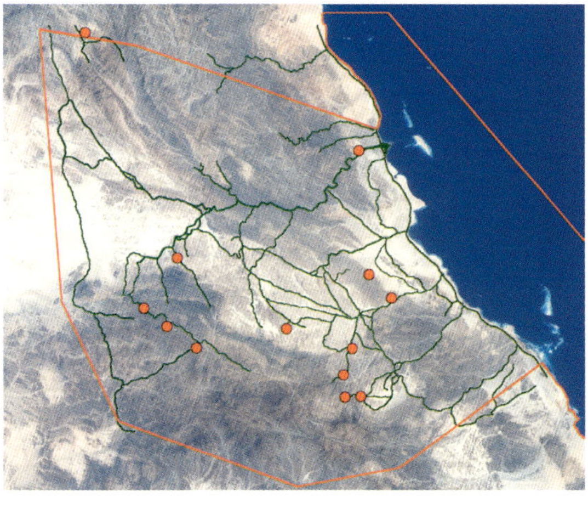

Leptadenia pyrotechnica

(Forssk.) Decne., 1838 (Asclepiadaceae)

Common local name: (Markh) مرخ

Description: An erect, compact, and dense shrub. Much-branched, up to 3 meters high, with cylindrical whip-like stems and clear bitter juice. Leafless, or with few linear leaves. Flowers yellow-green, on lateral umbellate, pubescent cymes.

Importance and uses: Grazing for camels and wild animals. Fruits and young twigs may be eaten by some local people. Fibers used in rope-making. In India the bruised stem and leaves are used to promote healing of wounds.

Ecology and distribution: A typical species found on sandy desert. Flowering from August to December and bearing fruit from November to March. Recorded in Wadi El Gemal, Hilifi, and Hamata.

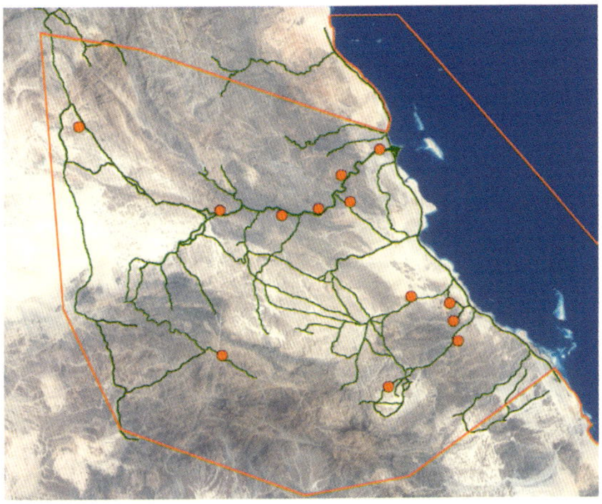

Limonium axillare

(Forssk.) Kuntze, 1891 (Plumbaginaceae)

Common English name: Sea lavender
Common local name: (Shalil) شليل
Description: A low shrub with erect stem. Old branches usually covered with the basal part of dead leaves. Leaves oblanceolate, coriaceous, and glabrous. A rose-purplish inflorescence.
Importance and uses: Decoction of the root bark used locally for diabetes. Elsehwere, as in the United Arab Emirates, its antibacterial and antifungal properties are used to treat wounds and inflammation.
Ecology and distribution: Preferring a saline habitat, it is abundant along the coast of the National Park and in desert depressions, as in the Wadi El Gemal delta, Sharm al-Luli, and Umm al-ʻAbas.

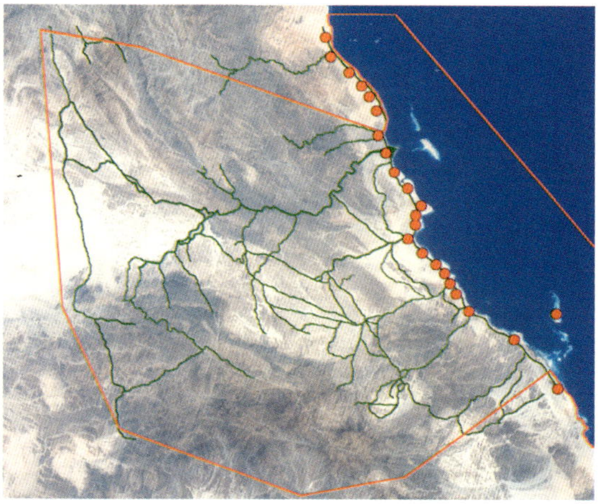

Lindenbergia indica

(L.) Vatke, 1875 (Scrophulariacea)

Common local name: ('Ud al-zughut) عود الزغط

Description: A perennial low shrub that grows up to 20–50 cm high, with woody base. Stem erect, with spreading branches; stem, branches, and leaves covered by glandular hair. Leaves broadly ovate, dentate, and rounded or truncate at base. Leaf-like bracts. Uppermost leaves shorter than the calyx. Orange and yellow flowers in lax, spike-like racemes.

Importance and uses: Grazing, mainly for wild animals, especially in dry seasons. No known local medicinal value. In India it is used for skin eruptions, chronic bronchitis, sore throat, toothache.

Ecology and distribution: Grows in stony wadis and hillsides and on cliffs. Recorded in Hilifi, Hulus, Hakrahub, and Sartut.

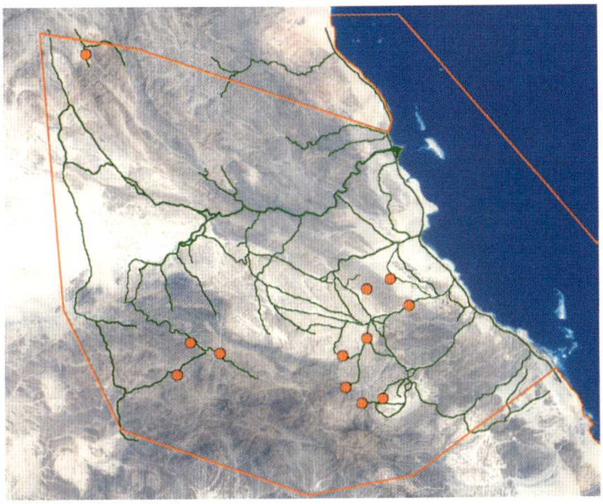

Lotononis platycarpa

(Viv.) Pichi-Serm., 1950 (Leguminosa)

Common local name: ('Ishib) عشب

Description: An annual dwarf herb covered by appressed hairs. Leaves minute, consisting of three smaller leaflets. Flowers small, cream-colored and in clusters. Legume very small, about 6 mm long, containing eight reniform seeds.

Importance and uses: One of the most important grazing plants during the rainy season. Collected locally for domestic animals, three to four months after rain or flood. No local medicinal value.

Ecology and distribution: Common all over the Park, forming very large green mats in sandy plains. Recorded in Wadi El Gemal, Abu Ghusun, Hankurab, and Hafafit.

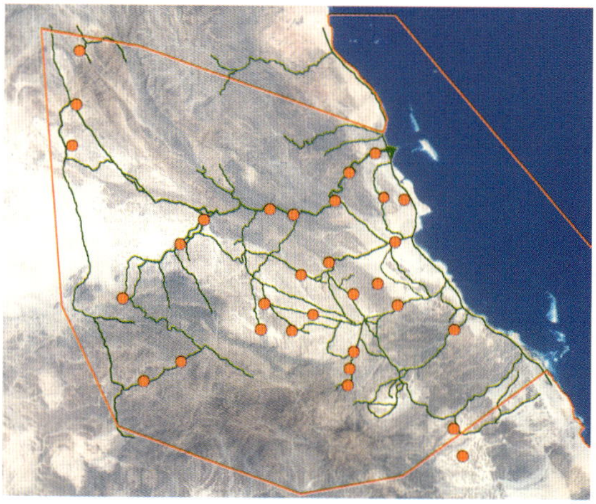

Lotus glinoides

Delile, 1837(Leguminosa)

Common local name: (Gudayb) قضيب

Description: An annual herb up to 10–25 cm high, gray-pubescent and smaller than *Lotus hebranicus*. Stem mainly procumbent, branching from the base. Leaves five pinnate, the lower pair of leaflets much smaller than the others. Flowers pale purple to white and forming an umbel. Legume up to 2 cm long, containing six to fifteen brown seeds.

Importance and uses: Edible for animals, but believed locally to be very harmful for domestic animals if grazed before sun rise: many cases of goats' deaths are attributed to this.

Ecology and distribution: Grows in sandy plains and desert wadis. Rare in the Park. Recorded in Hankurab.

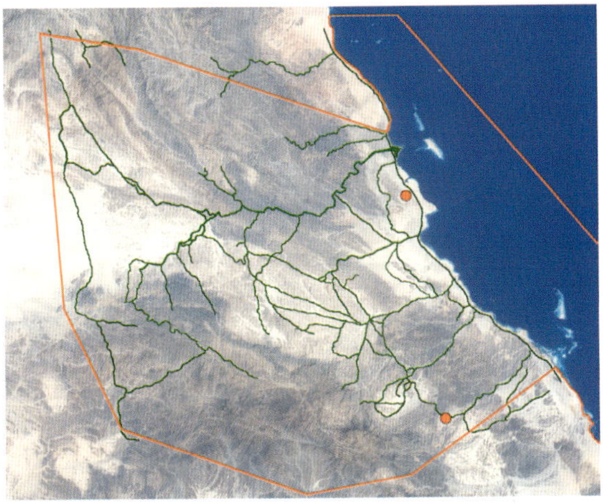

Lotus hebranicus

Hochst., 1898 (Leguminosa)

Common local name: (Gadub) قضب

Description: An annual or short-lived perennial shrublet up to 80 cm high. Branches ascending or procumbent; the entire plant is glabrous. Leaves five pinnate, the leaf rachis flattened. Flowers pink. Legume thick, straight, up to 4 cm long, with up to 25 seeds.

Importance and uses:

Edible for animals, but believed locally to be very harmful for domestic animals if grazed before sun rise. No local medicinal value but investigations prove that it contains many active properties.

Ecology: Grows in sandy plains and desert wadis. Common in the Park. Recorded in Wadi El Gemal, Abu Ghusun, and Hankurab.

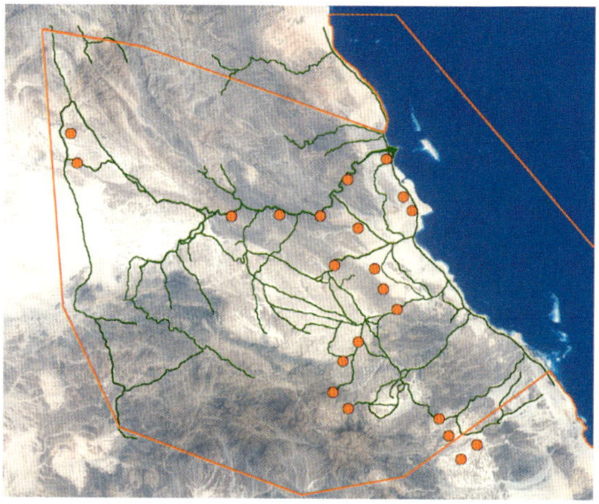

Lycium shawii

Roem. and Schult., 1819 (Solanacea)

Common English name: Desert thorn

Common local name: (Sahanun) سهانون

Description: A rounded, profusely spiny shrub. Shoots short, with terminal spine and clusters of leaves and one flower. Pale-violet flowers and orange-red fruits. Often cropped into stunted shapes by domestic animals; the only specimens that thrive are those that grow between the protecting branches of the Acacia. Interestingly, shows very fast growth after the rainy season.

Importance and uses: An important grazing plant, but shepherds are careful to avoid certain times when it becomes lethal for goats, especially at the beginning of branching after rain. In Tanzania the roots are boiled and the decoction used to treat sores in the mouth; in Somalia and Kenya it is used to treat coughs. The decoction is applied externally to relieve backache and to wash polio patients; cures tick fever in livestock.

Ecology and distribution: Grows in stony desert and wadis. Recorded all over the Park but more common in Abu Ghusun and Wadi El Gemal.

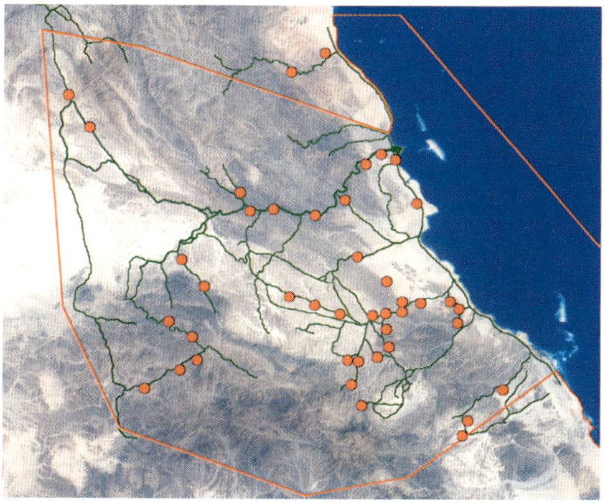

Maerua crassifolia

Forssk., 1775 (Capparaceae)

Common local name: (Sarh) سرح

Description: An evergreen tree or shrub up to 6 m high, umbrella shaped. Branches often spinescent. Leaves solitary on young branches, in clusters on old ones. Flowers in clusters, without petals. Pale green fruits.

Importance and uses: Used as firewood and for making kitchen tools because its wood is light. Leaves and fruits palatable to livestock. The sweet fruits also used for human consumption. Also used to treat domestic animals. The leaves are used as a febrifuge. The decoction of leaves is used in toothache and intestinal diseases. Locally believed to avert bad spell rituals and remove curses, a belief that occurs in many African tribes.

Ecology and distribution: Grows well in sandy plains, stony wadis and slopes. Recorded only in the western part of the Park, as in Hafafit, Hangaliya, and Abu Hamamid.

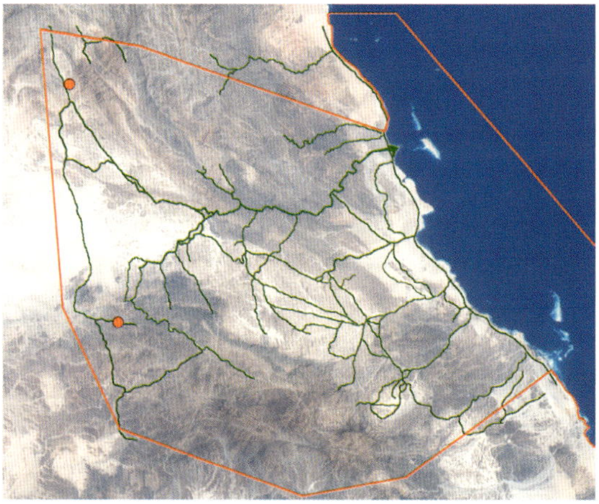

Malva parviflora

L., 1753 (Malvaceae)

Common English name: Cheese weed, Egyptian mallow
Common local name: (Khubbayza) خبيزة
Description: A stout, bushy annual or short-lived perennial herb with branching and spreading from the base, and short thick root. Large, soft leaves, alternate, almost circular, usually five to seven shallow lobes. White flowers, solitary or a few in dense cymes. Seeds enclosed in a rounded disk.
Importance and uses: Grazing. Young leaves are gathered before the appearance of the flowers and cooked in soups or with butter, oil, and salt. Leaves have high mineral content. Roots are chewed for pyorrhea. Infusion of flowering and fruiting parts has astringent properties. Many recent drugs incorporate the name *Malva*, as there are many *Malva* derivatives.
Ecology and distribution: Cultivated in the Nile delta for consumption, but not common in the Park. Recorded in Wadi El Gemal and al-Ludayyid.

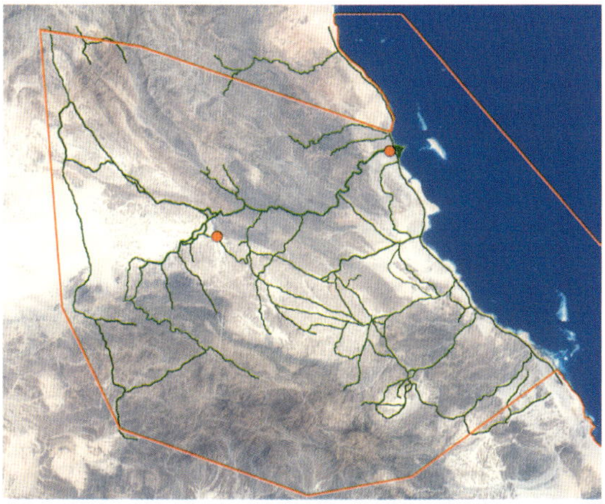

Morettia philaeana

(Delile) DC., 1821 (Crucifera)

Common local name: (Taghar) تغر

Description: A perennial, yellowish-green herb. Tomentose, with scabrous brittle stellate hairs that are readily detached and adhere to fingers. Stem 20–80 cm long, ascending or prostrate and often forming thick mats of several layers on mud flats. Leaves oblong-elliptic with short petiole. Flowers white and yellow inside, with hairy sepals. Siliqua (fruit) are tetragonous (four-angled), straight or slightly curved, appressed to the stem.

Importance and uses: Grazing. No known medicinal value.

Ecology and distribution: Rare in the Park. Recorded only on the western boundaries of the Park, in al-Nuhud and ‘Antar.

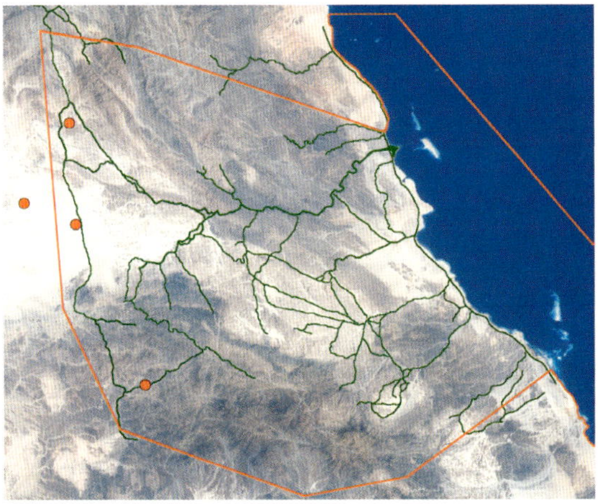

Moringa peregrina

(Forssk.) Fiori, (1911) (Moringaceae)

Common English name: Ben-oil tree

Common local name: (Maya) مايا

Description: A tree up to 10 m high, with erect trunk and white bark. Leaves about 30 cm long, each formed of three pairs of long, slender pinnae. The naked leaf axis remains, giving the tree a wispy look similar to *Tamarix* sp. Flowers pinkish white, appearing in May before the leaves. Pod pendulous, with angled, nut-like seeds (behen nuts) of bitter sweet taste and rich in oil.

Importance and uses: No local experience of the benefits of *M. pergrina*, yet many studies confirm its importance. Good-quality oil (ben oil) is obtained from the seeds. It is thought this may have been one of the important oils used by the ancient Egyptians for preparing cosmetics. Today, many Sudanese tribes use suspensions of seed powder to effectively clarify even turbid water . An excellent source of protein, vitamins, and minerals, especially the leaves.

Ecology and distribution: Confined to mountain foothills higher than 700 m above sea level. Recorded in Sartut, Hangaliya, and the Hamata mountains.

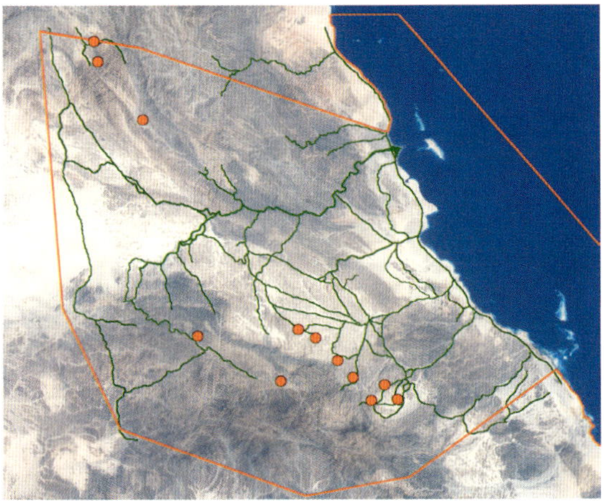

Neurada procumbens

L., 1753 (Nuradaceae)

Common English name: Creeping thorn rose

Common local name: (Sa'dan) سعدان

Description: A prostrate, gray-green, densely tomentose annual herb. Branching stems radiating from the base. Leaves ovate-lanceolate in outline. Flowers inconspicuous, short-pedicelled in the upper axils. Petals cream, greenish or pinkish colored. Fruit flat, discoid, 1.2–2 cm in diameter, hardening and woody at maturity, smooth and flat below, convex with prickles above.

Importance and uses: Grazing is locally believed to produce the best milk. Young fruits and fresh leaves eaten locally. Bedouin use it traditionally as a medicinal herb. Modern studies prove that its aqueous extract increases blood pressure.

Ecology and distribution: Grows after rain in sandy plains, the fruit spines attaching it to sheep wool, which helps to disperse it. Recorded in Abu Ghusun, Wadi El Gemal, and Hulus.

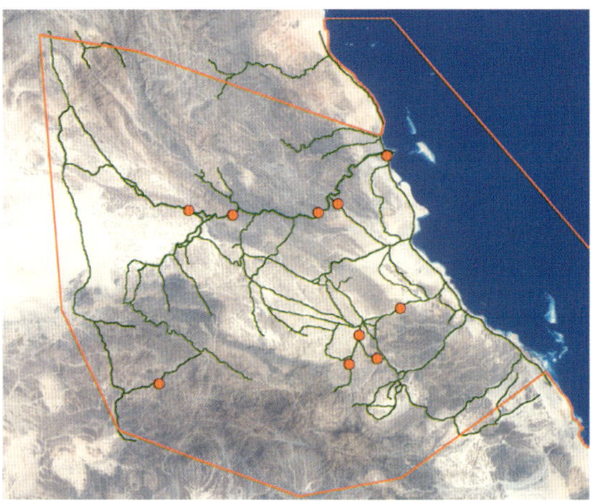

Nitraria retusa

Forssk., 1778 (Nitrariaceae)

Common local name: (Ghargad) غرقد

Description: An erect, much-branched, armed or unarmed perennial shrub. Leaves alternate, simple, fleshy, and of bitter taste. Retuse or dentate at the apex. Flowers white, in loose cymes. Flowering takes place at the beginning of spring. Fruits fleshy drupes, and red.

Importance and uses: An important natural sand controller. Leaves and twigs occasionally grazed by sheep, goats, and camels. Fleshy red fruits edible for humans and birds, said to be useful in the treatment of urinary tract disorders.

Ecology and distribution: Confined to salt marshes, where it forms saline mounds that stud the flat ground. Recorded in Wadi El Gemal Delta.

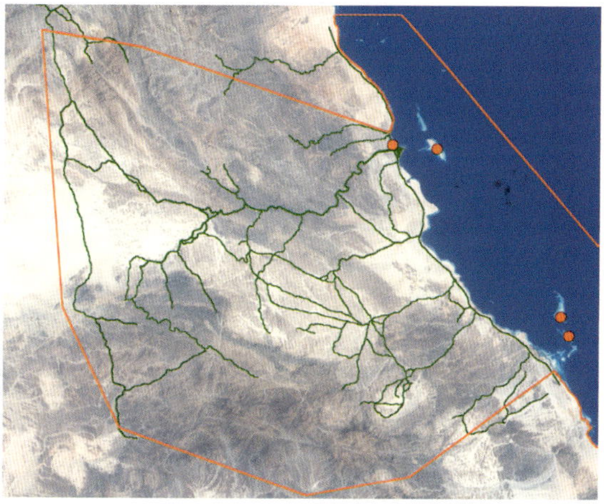

Ochradenus baccatus

Delile, 1814 (Resedaceae)

Common English name: Pearl plant

Common local name: (Gurdi) قرضى

Description: A perennial dioecious shrub, often spinescent. Mainly procumbent but may also climb Acacia trees. Leaves linear, soon caducous. Male flowers yellow, in racemes without petals. Female flowers have tuberculate seeds. The majority of angiosperms have a single annual bout of reproduction; species that flower continually throughout the year are rare. *Ochradenus baccatus* is a gynodioecious, desert shrub whose principal flowering period is associated with the winter rains, although large individuals also remain in flower during the hot dry summer. (Right, third photograph down: male flowers. Right, bottom: female flowers.)

Importance and uses: Grazing. The main food for the Ocellated Dab Lizard *(Uromastyx ocellata)*. Flavonoids have been isolated from the aerial parts.

Ecology and distribution: Grows in stony wadis and hilly slopes. Recorded many times climbing on Acacia trees. Recorded in Hulus, Wadi El Gemal, and Hilifi.

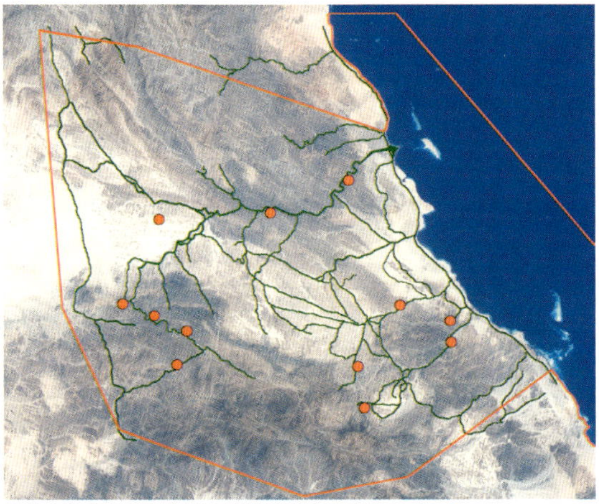

Orobanche cernua

Loefl., 1758 (Orbanchaceae)

Common English name: Broomrape
Common local name: (Haluk) هالوك
Description: A puberulent biennial or short perennial parasitic plant. Devoid of chlorophyll and unable to synthesize its own nutriment, it is a parasite on roots of different herbs or shrubs, mainly on species of Solanaceae like *Lycium shawii*. Stem grows up to 40 cm high, and slightly swollen at base; more or less glandular-hairy. Scales broadly deltoid to lanceolate and acuminate. Flowers sessile, in dense spike. Corolla tube white and glossy, the limb short and blue.
Importance and uses: Grazing. No local medicinal or economic value recorded. Recent studies prove that *O. cernua* extract displays remarkable activity against some gram-positive bacteria such as Streptococcus and Staphylococcus.
Ecology and distribution: Grows in sandy and alluvial soils. Rare in the Park. Recorded only in al-Khashir.

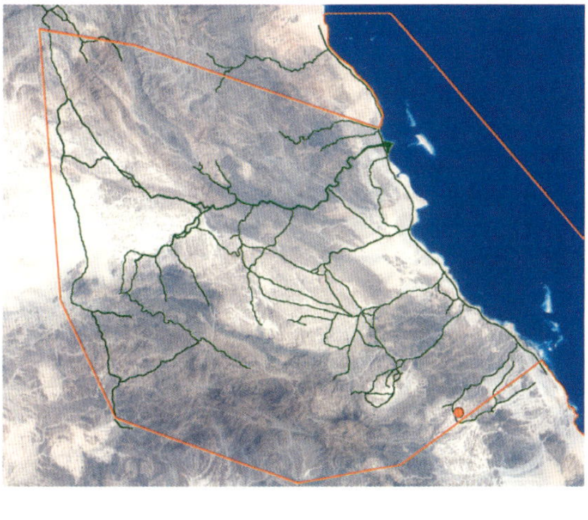

Panicum turgidum

Forssk., 1775 (Gramineae)

Common English name: Turgid panic grass
Common local name: (Shush) شوش
Description: A perennial grass. High tolerance to drought conditions, good level of nutritive value, regarded as an effective species for sand dune fixation. Pale green. Forms rounded bushes.

Many cylindrical hollow stems (culms) arise from the base, branched at the nodes. Leaf-blades linear, rolled, pungent, and much shorter than the sheath. Flowers and seeds in panicle inflorescence. Not all flowers are fertile.
Importance and uses: Seeds collected locally for cooking. Considered one of the important grazing species, especially in dry regions. In other regions local inhabitants may chew the plant for treating toothache and use the extract of the plant in treating wounds and removing spots on the eye.
Ecology and distribution: Grows well in sandy plains. Recorded in Wadi El Gemal, Abu Ghusun, Hafafit, and Hamata. (Right, top: during the dry season. Right, center and bottom: 3 months after the rain event.)

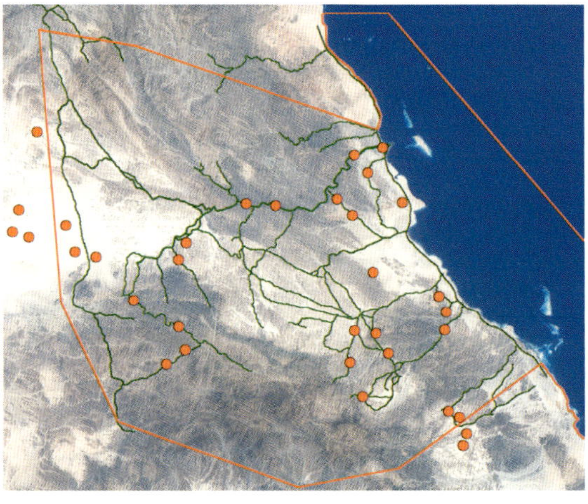

Pergularia tomentosa

L., 1767 (Asclepiadaceae)

Common local name: (Ghalga) غلقة

Description: A gray-green shrub with milky sap, completely covered by short hairs. Young branches roll up around the old branches. Leaves green, heart-shaped. Inflorescences in small bunches, white yellowish, green-brownish, with hairy edges.

Fruits are lengthened follicules, hooked towards the apex and covered with soft prickles. With maturity, the fruits open and let seeds escape with brushes of white hairs.

Importance and uses: Grazing. Also used for tanning, crushed and spread out over animal hides. This plant produces a corrosive milk-like secretion, and when touched can discolor the skin. Also used to counteract snake bites. Plant acts as lactation stimulants in animals. Plant latex used as a depilatory. Root used in pulmonary troubles. Sap used to cure cutaneous and subcutaneous parasitic infections.

Ecology and distribution: Grows in stony hillsides. Recorded in al-Ludayyid, al-Nuhud, Umm al-'Abas, and Hafafit.

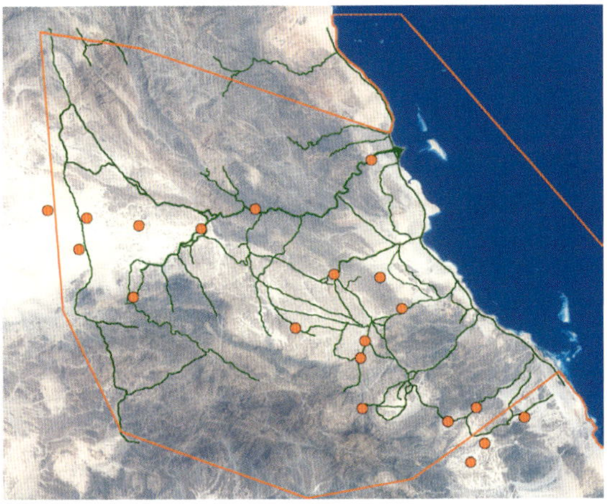

Periploca angustifolia

Labill., 1791 (Asclepiadaceae)

Common English name: Wolf bane
Common local name: (Murrikh) مريخ
Description: A perennial shrub with numerous compact, glabrous branches. Leaves opposite, sessile, and entire. Flowers purple inside and violet towards the tip, with five purple, filamentous, curled corolla segments. Flowers have a central white fluffy stigma. The fruit is an opposite pair of narrow, horn-like follicles with pointed, slightly curved apex. Each follicle holds numerous seeds with tufts of long, silk-like hairs at one end to aid seed dispersion in the wind.
Importance and uses: Grazing. No known medicinal properties.
Ecology and distribution: Grows in high altitude stony wadis. A very restricted distribution in the Park. Recorded in the high tributaries of Abu Ghusun, Rumit, and on the Hilifi side of the Hamata mountains.

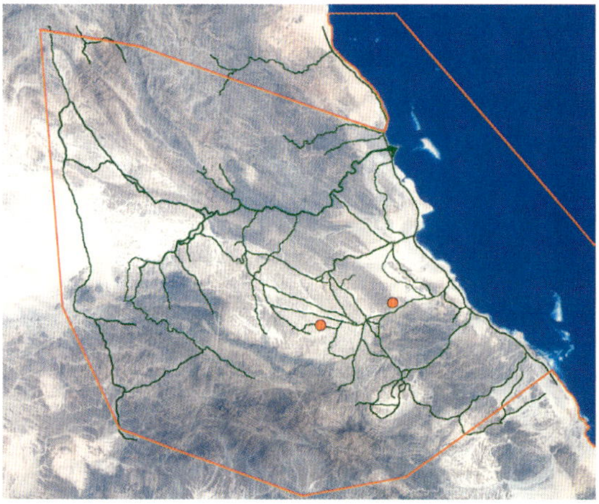

Phoenix dactylifera

L., 1753 (Palmae)

Common English name: Date-palm

Common local name: (Nakhl) نخل

Description:A tall, erect, regularly cylindrical, unbranched tree with a crown of huge, compound leaves. The sheath and petiole of the leaf very often with stout spines. Dioecious male and female flowers found in individual plants of the same species. The fruit, a hard seed enclosed by a sweet fleshy shell, yellow or red when ripe, turning to black or brown.

Importance and uses: Fresh fruit (date) edible, or can be dried and preserved. Trunks provide valuable building material. The durable leaves are used for thatching and as weaving material. The leaf base has a fibrous tuft used for scrubbing and cleaning.

Ecology and distribution: Not common in the Park. Some 90 specimens in the Wadi El Gemal delta.

(Center, left: female flowers. Center, right: male flowers.)

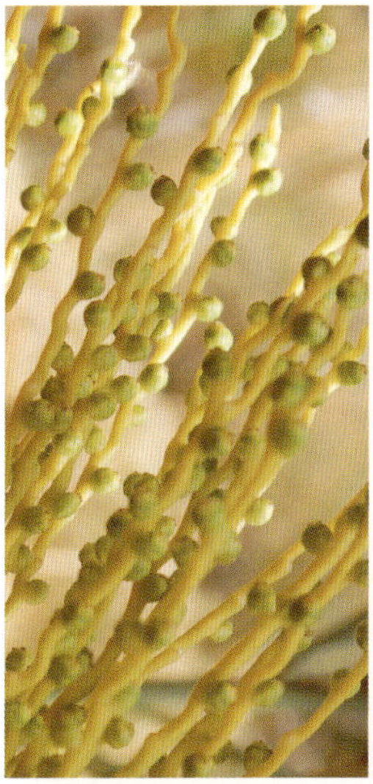

Phragmites australis

(Cav.) Trin., 1841 (Gramneae)

Common English name: Common reed

Common local name: (Bus) بوص

Description: A wetland reed grass species with woody hollow culms, up to 3.5 meters high, with gray-green leaves. Large masses of brown flower branches. These rarely produce seeds, and become fluffy, gray masses. Capable of reproducing by seed, but does so primarily by means of rhizomes.

Importance and uses: Grazing. Parts of the stem eaten locally raw. High quality forage. In Russia they are harvested and processed into starch. The leaves are used in the treatment of bronchitis and cholera, the ash of the leaves is applied to infected sores.

Ecology and distribution: Grows in any open, wet area, such as in the Wadi El Gemal delta around a small brackish lake of salt water and fresh flood water. Also recorded in Sartut, around some ponds formed during floods.

Plantago amplexicaulis

Cav., 1793 (Plantaginaceae)

Common local name: (Hulagayt) هولاقيت

Description: An eglandular-hairy annual herb, about 10–40 cm high. Stem short, simple or sparsely branched, and terete. Leaves much longer than stem, alternate, with wide sheathing base, linear to oblanceolate, petiolate and entire. Peduncle erect or ascending and much longer than leaves. Flowers in spikes, which are ovoid to short-cylindrical.

Importance and uses: Grazing. No other local use. But it is documented that the dried seeds are demulcent, febrifuge, ophthalmic, and pectoral. They are used in the treatment of intestinal complaints. Seeds contain up to 30 percent mucilage, which swells up in the gut, acting as a bulk laxative and soothing irritated membranes.

Ecology and distribution: Grows in sandy and alluvial soil in wadis and desert plains. Rare in the Park. Recorded in al-Khashir, Hulus, and Hangaliya.

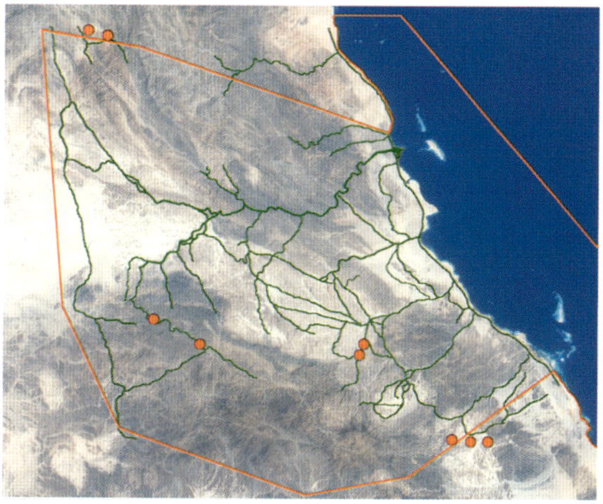

Plantago ciliata

Desf., 1798 (Plantaginaceae)

Common English name: Small mountain plantain

Common local name: (Hulagayt) هولاقيت

Description: An annual herbaceous plant with very short stem. Small, about 10–15 cm high, densely villous. Stem rarely branched. Leaves in rosette, with wide clasping base, hairy and narrow lanceolate. Flowers small, greenish, in globose spikes. Contains high amounts of gelatinous compounds and is very rich in water.

Importance and uses: Grazing. The spikes are collected and added to milk to improve the milk's quality and edibility. In other regions, considered a desert survival plant for its water content. Aerial parts used for veterinary purposes.

Ecology and distribution: Grows in sandy and stony wadis. Recorded in Hafafit, Hangaliya, al-Khashir, and Abu Ghusun.

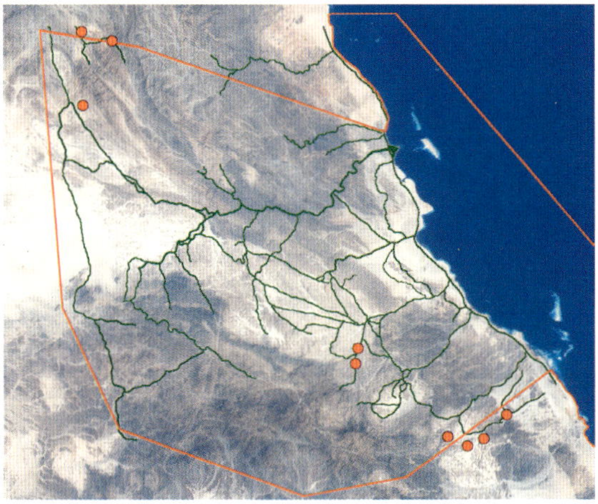

Plantago exigua

Murray, 1779 (Plantaginaceae)

Common local name: (Swigat) سويقات

Description: A sparsely glandular-hairy, annual herb. Stem branched from the base. Branches ascending and terete. Leaves opposite, linear and entire, or with a few small irregular teeth. Apical peduncles shorter than leaves. Spikes ovoid and lax below. Corolla glabrous with apiculate lobes. Capsules are two-seeded.

Importance and uses: Grazing. No other local use.

Ecology and distribution: Grows in sandy and alluvial soil. Rare in the Park. Recorded in Hangaliya, Wadi El Gemal, Hulus, al-Khashir, and Sartut.

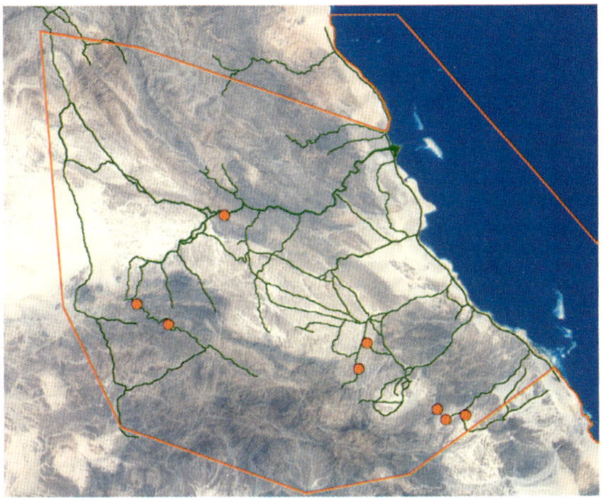

Pulicaria incisa

(Lam.) DC., 1836 (Compsitae)

Common local name: (Rabul) ربل

Other common names: (Shay al-jabal) شاى الجبل

Description: A short-lived, perennial herb. Much-branched, woolly. Stem erect, branched mainly from the base. Strongly undulate and dentate leaves. Flowers yellow, forming solitary capitula, or a few together, in open cymose.

Importance and uses: Grazing. It has an aromatic scent and a tisane is brewed from it (in Arabic *Shay al-jabal* means 'tea of the mountain'). It is a stimulant and anti-flatulent. Recently, bioactive lipids and anti-oxidant have been isolated from it, and it is now sought by the pharmaceutical industry for use as a traditional herbal tea.

Ecology and distribution: Grows in desert wadis, sandy and alluvial habitats. Common in the Park. Recorded in Wadi El Gemal and Abu Ghusun, and in Wadi al-Abyad it appears as a green woolly mat.

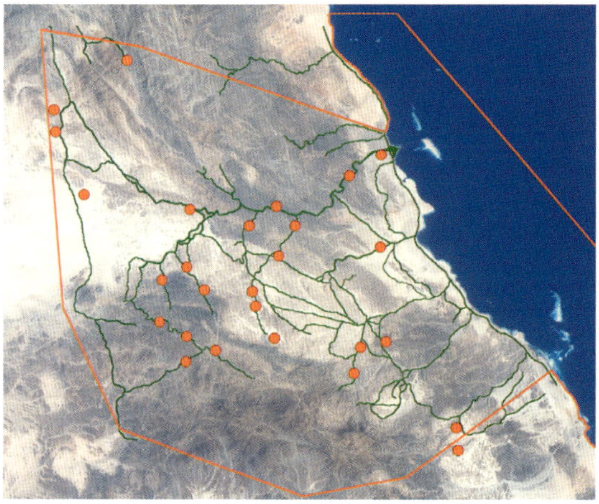

Pulicaria undulata subsp. *undulata*

(L.) Mey, 1831 (Compsitae)

Common English name: Crisp-leaved fleabane

Common local name: (Jitya) جيتيا

Description: A low perennial shrub, often cushion-shaped, up to 60 cm high. Much-branched, the juvenile branches are densely white-appressed and woolly. Leaves oblong, sessile, with undulated margins (hence the name, *undulata*). Flowers yellow, in terminal cymes forming capitula (enlarged and rounded heads). Flowers March to June.

Importance and uses: Grazing, especially when alternatives are rare. Fumes from burning are used to treat measles and repel insects. Aerial parts contain essential oils that have a characteristic aroma and have exhibited antibacterial activities.

Ecology and distribution: Grows in desert wadis, sandy and alluvial habitats. Recorded in Wadi El Gemal, Hafafit, and Abu Ghusun.

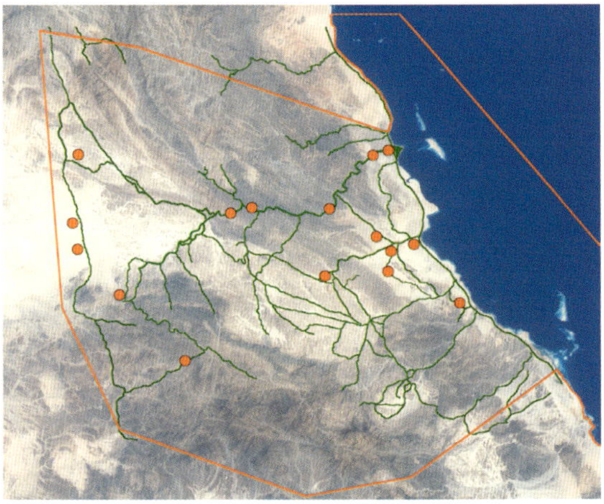

Reichardia tingitana

(L.) Roth, 1787 (Compsitae)

Common local name: (Hiwwi' al-kilab) هويع الكلاب

Description: An annual, glabrescent herb, about 5–50 cm high and papillose-scabrid. Leaves fleshy with minutely prickly margins and set in a basal rosette. Basal leaves toothed to pinnatifid, oblanceolate and narrowed at base. Florets golden yellow with a purple base. Achenes 1.5–2.5 mm long, pale; the inner ones commonly aborted.

Importance and uses: Grazing. No other local medicinal use. Believed to be eaten by dogs (hence its local name). Recently new contact toxic compounds and antifeedants (agent that causes a pest to stop eating) have been isolated from its aerial parts.

Ecology and distribution: Grows in desert wadis and alluvial plains. Recorded in Wadi El Gemal, Abu Ghusun, and Hulus.

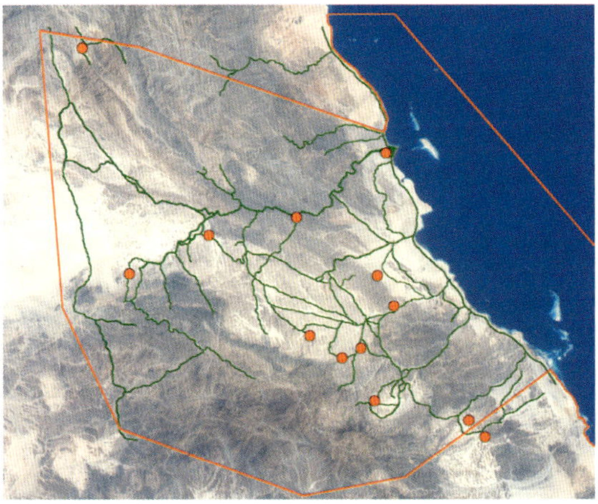

Reseda pruinosa

Delile, 1814 (Resedaceae)

Common English name: Reseda

Common local name: (Khuzama) خزامة

Description: An annual herb up to 70 cm high. Lower leaves entire, upper leaves ternately divided or pinnatisect. Stems and branches carry projecting papillae formed by much-dilated epidermal cells. Flowers small, white, and in dense long terminal racemes up to 30 cm long. The name pruinose is related to the white powder-like structure that covers stems and branches. Seeds enclosed in capsules of about 1 cm long.

Importance and uses: Good pasture. No other known local use. Recently flavonoids have been isolated from the aerial parts.

Ecology and distribution Common during the rainy season, easy to distinguish the long racemes in any sandy or gravelly plain. Recorded in Hangaliya, Wadi El Gemal, Kabb al-Khawwara, and Abu Ghusun.

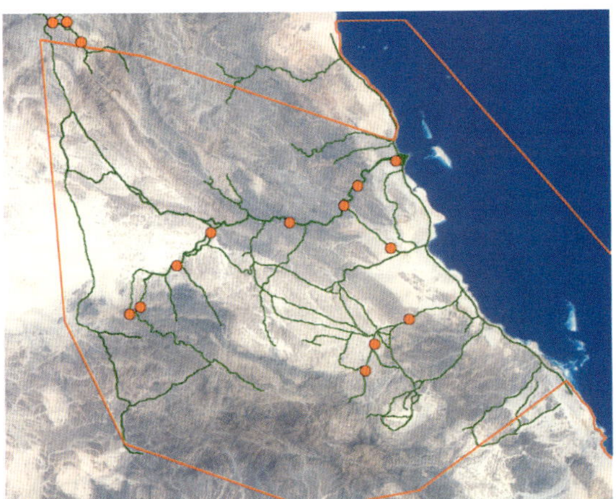

Rhus tripartita

(Ucria) Grande, 1918 (Anacardiaceae)

Common local name: (Dablut) دبلوت

Description: A dioecious, woody perennial shrub with short and spiny branches. Stem mainly reddish brown and glossy. Leaves three-foliate. Leaflets sessile and with dentate margins. Flowers minute, greenish-yellow, in axillary or terminal panicles. Drupe (fruit) is greenish, becoming red on ripening, glossy and glabrous.

Importance and uses: The fruit is edible. An infusion of fruit and leaves is used for gastric and intestinal ailments. In other regions inhalation of the vapors released from stems in boiling water treats head cold. Bark used for dyeing and tanning.

Ecology and distribution: Grows on rocks, mainly in foothills. Rare and endangered. Recorded in Sartut, Hakrahub, and Hilifi.

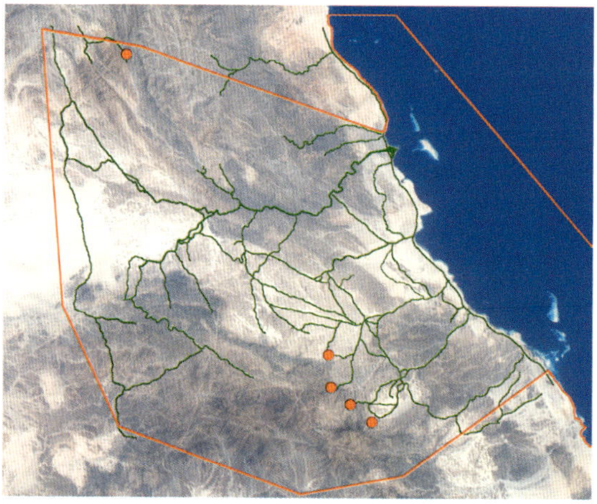

Rumex vesicarius

L., 1753 (Polygonaceae)

Common English name: Indian Sorrel, Bladder dock
Common local name: (Hummad) حماض
Description: An annual, glabrous herb, with erect to ascending stem and branching from base. Juicy stems and leaves. Leaves fleshy and with long petiols. Flowers bisexual, greenish to purplish. Fruits winged, entire, and purplish-red-veined. Flowers March to April.
Importance and uses: Leaves eaten raw locally. The acid-lemon flavor comes from high levels of oxalic acid. In other regions it is used for constipation, bad digestion, and as an appetizer. Stomachic, diuretic, and astringent. The roasted seeds are eaten for the cure of dysentery. The plant juice is used to check toothache and nausea and to promote appetite.
Ecology and distribution: Grows in sandy and stony habitats. Recorded in Wadi El Gemal, Hulus, Hangaliya, and Abu Ghusun.

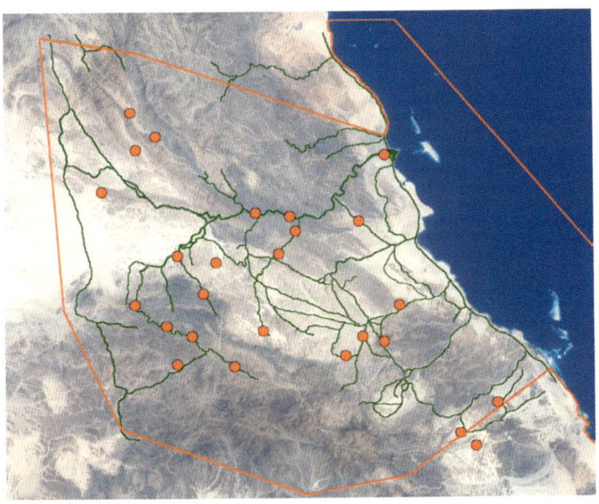

Salsola imbricata

Forssk., 1775 (Chenopodiaceae)

Common local name: (Khrayt) خريط

Description: A subshrub or small shrub, densely branched, 0.3–1.2 m high. Stems and lower leaves densely covered with spreading or ascending, warty hairs. Branches reddish brown when young, ascending with regularly arranged, spreading lateral, catkin-like spikes. Leaves succulent, with flat to convex surface and linear to narrow triangular lower parts. Decayed, it has a fishy smell when squeezed.

Importance and uses: Grazing for camels. No other local medicinal or economic value. In other regions used in producing alkaline compounds.

Ecology and distribution: Not common in the Park; recorded in Umm al-'Abas only. But outside the Park dominant in Wadi Khrayt (hence its name).

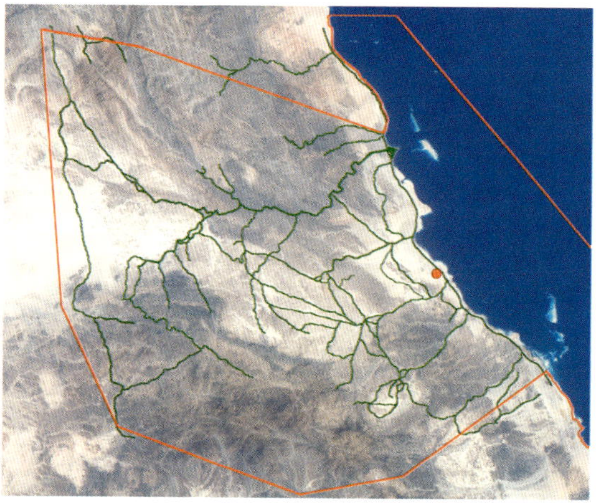

Salvadora persica

L., 1753 (Salvadoraceae)

Common local name: (Arak) اراك

Other common names: (Siwak) سواك (branches and roots)

Description: Arak is an evergreen shrub up to 5 m high, often forming impenetrable thickets. Glabrous, with white branches. Leaves opposite, oblong, and with short petioles. Racemes form a spike-like panicle. Small, spherical white fruits that change to red then black at maturity.

Importance and uses: It has a religious value for all Muslims who use *siwak* five times a day to clean teeth. In addition to its grazing value, local people pick and eat the fruits. The pieces of the underground stolons, or runners, and sometimes the branches, are all known as *siwak*, and are used for brushing teeth and as an oral antiseptic. Boiled leaves are used to treat urinary tract pain. The dried fruits' powder is diuretic. Some companies produce toothpaste preparations containing extract of arak, called 'miswak' or 'siwak.'

Ecology and distribution: Grows in sandy wadis and on cliffs. Recorded in Wadi El Gemal, al-Ghadir, and in Wadi El Gemal Island.

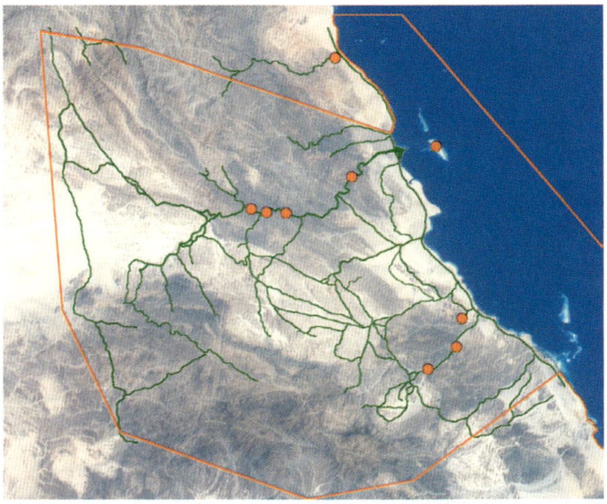

Salvia aegyptiaca

L., 1753 (Labiateae)

Common English name: Egyptian sage

Common local name: (Ibsiwi) إبسوى

Description: A much-branched herb, woody at base. Stems above and below angular, with short or longer hairs. Leaves narrow and linear-elliptical. Flowering stalks up to 5 mm. Calyx bell-shaped, enlarging in fruit, with a prominent covering of hairs. Corolla pale lilac. Upper lip fairly broad, lower lip longer than the upper. May survive four years in dry conditions.

Importance and uses: Grazing. No local medicinal use. In other regions it is used to treat various unrelated conditions, such as nervous disorders, dizziness, trembling, and diarrhoea. Recent studies show that its methanolic extract has strong antimicrobial and antioxidant effects.

Ecology and distribution: Grows in stony habitats, with good growth and yield in foothills. Recorded in Hangaliya, Hulus, al-Ludayyid and once in Wadi El Gemal.

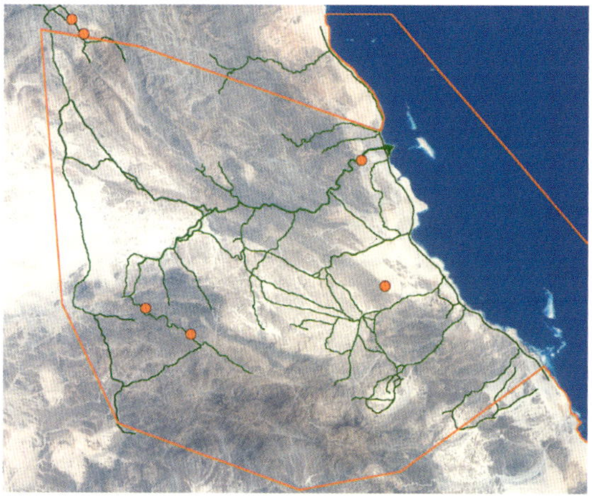

Sarcocornia fruticosa

(L.) A.J. Scott, Bot. J. Soc. 75:367 (1977).
(Chenopodiaceae)

Common English name: Shrubby swamp fire; Glasswort
Common local name: (Shunan) شنان
Description: An extensively branched bush, native to saline soils. Characterized by its young stems, fleshy and articulated in nodes, green or reddish. Leaves reduced to hardly visible small scales. Flowers grouped into threes per node of the fertile branches, which are the topmost and stand out from the general profile of the plant. Flowers small and only just apparent, and each one occupying a cavity in the stem. This species forms fertile branches without protruding above the general profile of the plant. It is at times confused with *Arthrocnemum macrostachyum*, which is of a very similar morphology and occupies the same habitat.
Importance and uses: The edible leaves have a brackish taste. A source of potash; used in soap-making. It has been recently proved that the aerial parts contain eremophilane derivatives which have industrial value.
Ecology and distribution: Common along the coast of the Park.

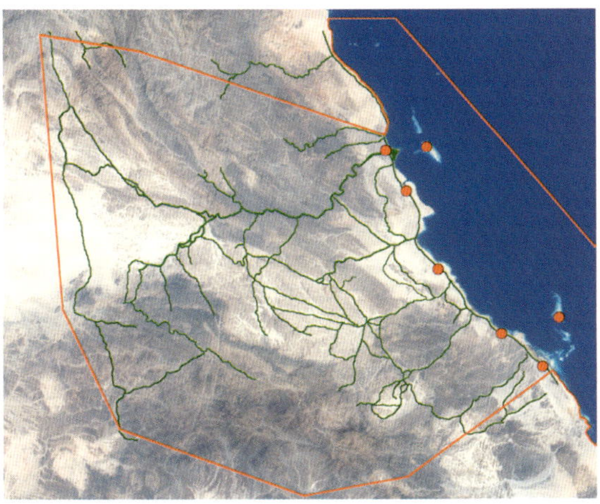

Senecio flavus

(Decne.) Sch.Bip., 1847 (Compositae)

Common local name: (Hadhadid) هدهديد

Description: An annual glabrous herb up to 35 cm. Stem erect with divaricating branching manner. Leaves dentate with the lower surface often reddish-violet. Lower leaves broadly ovate, the upper cordate, sessile, and clasping. Capitula in lax corymbose inflorescence, discoid or short-rayed. Seed usually attached by silky hairs, aiding in dispersal.

Importance and uses: Grazing. No other local use.

Ecology and distribution: Grows in sandy and stony desert wadis, giving good growth in the shade of big trees. Recorded in Wadi El Gemal, Hulus, and Abu Ghusun.

Senna alexandrina

Mill., 1768 (Leguinosa)

Common name: Tennevelly, Alexandrina senna

Common local name: (Sana Abbali) سنا أبالى

Description: A perennial low shrub up to 90 cm high, with compound paripinnate leaves. Leaflets are lanceolate, with the upper surface glabrous or almost so, and the lower more or less densely pubescent.

Flowers bright yellow, in erect, stalked, axillary and terminal racemes. Pods rounded at the apex, flat, falcate-oblong, pubescent when young and glabrous with age.

Importance and uses: A famous medicinal plant, one of the most extensively collected desert species. It yields most of the commercial Alexandria senna consumed in the country. The leaves are dried and boiled as a tea to act as a stimulant laxative, usually effective within six to twelve hours.

Ecology and distribution: Common in the Park, particularly in the western portion as in Hafafit, Natash, al-Nuhud; recorded also in Umm Sanayat and Wadi El Gemal.

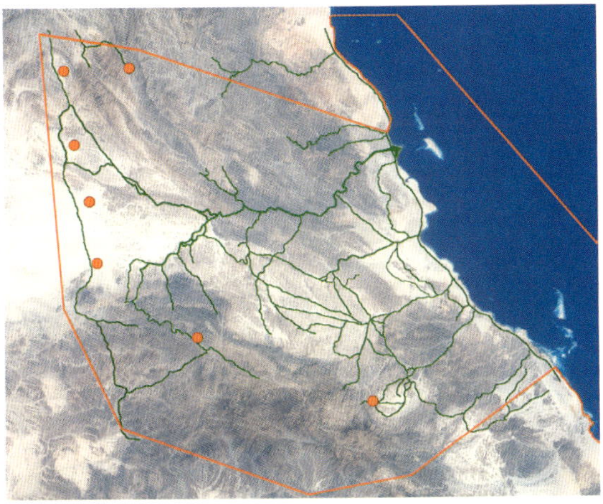

Senna italica

Mill., 1768 (Leguinosa)

Common English name: Mecca senna

Common local name: (Sanamikki) سنامكى

Description: A usually erect but sometimes ascending-spreading branched small shrub with dark green leaves, up to 1 m high. Leaves paripinnate with three to six pairs of obovate, obtuse, and mucronate leaflets. A yellow raceme with darker veined flowers. Pods flat, curved-oblong, and with a transverse series of creases.

Importance and uses: As for *Senna alexandrina*. Recent studies have identified new anthraquinone compounds exhibiting antibacterial properties and inhibiting tumor promotion induced by *Agrobacterium tumefaciens*.

Ecology and distribution: Grows mainly in the same habitats as *Senna alexandrina*. Recorded in Hafafit, Hangaliya, and al-Nikhira.

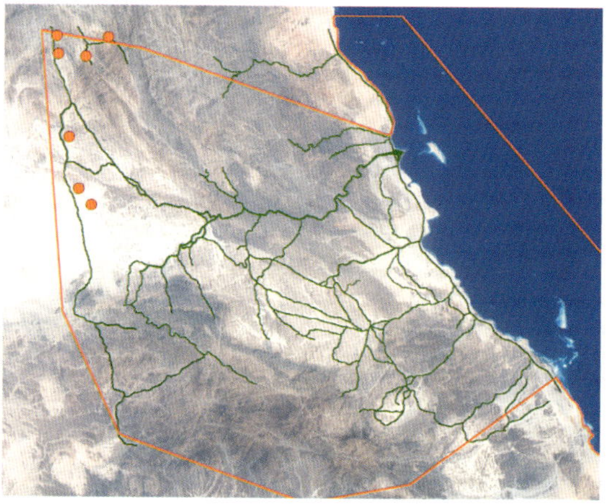

Silene linearis

Decne., 1835 (Caryophyllaceae)

Common local name: (Miswig) مسويق

Description: An annual plant but possibly biennial or even perennial in a favorable series of seasons. Up to 50 cm. Stem stiff with occasional branches which can be upright. Lower leaves linear, up to 1 cm long, clustered around the nodes; higher up they become progressively shorter. The pairs of leaves at the base of the flowering sterns are extremely small conspicuous flowers, with petals fused into a long tube. The white corolla is distinctively surrounded by parallel-veined sepals, an easily identifiable feature.

Importance and uses: Grazing. No other local value.

Ecology and distribution: Common on hillsides. Recorded in Hangaliya, Hilifi, and Hulus.

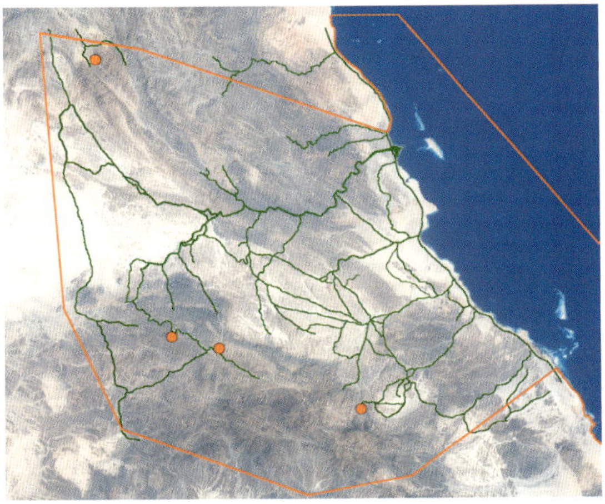

Solenostemma arghel

(Del.) Hayne, (1825) (Asclepiadaceae)

Common English name: Arghel

Common local name: (Hargal) حرجل

Description: An erect perennial undershrub up to 60 cm high. Leaves opposite, decussate, lanceolate, and with acute apex. Flowers white and in cymose inflorescence. Fruit a follicle, ovoid lanceolate and acuminate at the apex, very hard and dark purple at maturity. Seeds turgid, ovoid, bearing one apical tuft of hairs.

Importance and uses: Dried leaves are used for coughs. Infusion of leaves is used for gastro-intestinal cramps, stomach, colic, colds, and urinary tract problems. In Lebanon, boiled leaves in olive oil are used as a rub having antirheumatic properties. Leaves extract displays topical anti-inflammatory activity.

Ecology and distribution: The plant is endangered. It is heavily collected from its natural habitats for sale in *attarine* (herb shops) of traditional medicinal herbs all over Egypt. Grows on gravelly soil as in Nugrus, Gali, Wadi El Gemal, and Hangaliya.

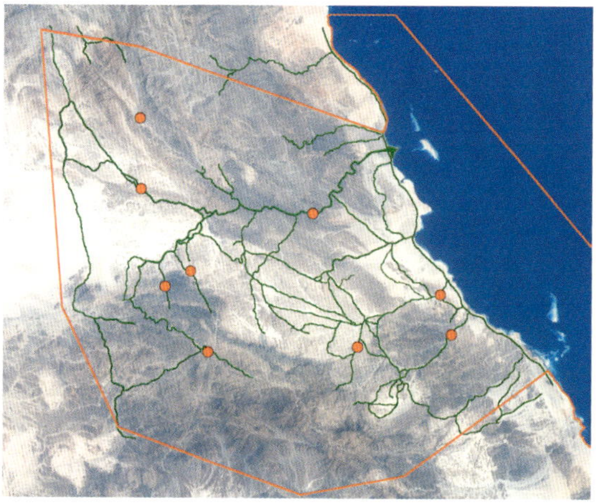

Suaeda monoica

Forssk., 1791 (Chenopodiaceae)

Common local name: (Suwwayda) سويدة

Description: A shrub or small tree up to 3 m in height. It has variability in growth form and size of individuals and leaves. Annual fruiting branches usually drooping. Dark green when living, black when dried. Young branches pale green or purplish, smooth. Leaves moderately to distinctly succulent, linear, and flattened or moderately convex on both sides. Inflorescences spike-like, terminating lateral branches, at base usually with female, at apex with male flowers. May contain bisexual flowers. Seeds black, shiny, and smooth.

Importance and uses: No local value. In other regions used as ointment for wounds. It has recently been shown that the extract of leaves displays antibacterial activity.

Ecology and distribution: Grows in moderately salty clay, coastal and inland sandy soil, and on edges of salt marshes. Recorded in Wadi El Gemal Island, Wadi El Gemal Delta, and Umm al-'Abas.

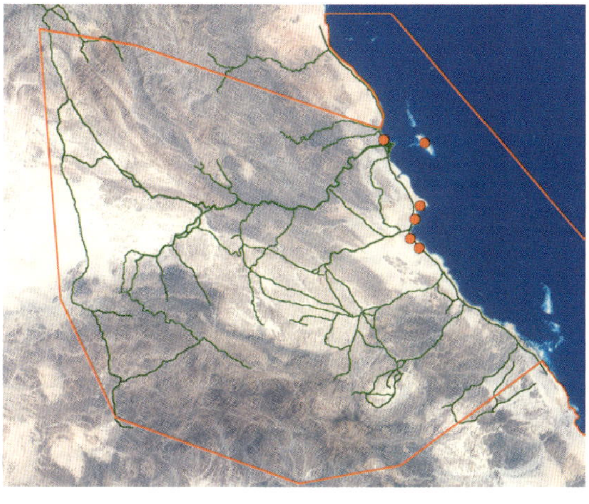

Tamarix aphylla

(L.) Karst., 1882 (Tamaricaceae)

Common English name: Tamarisk

Common local name: (Itl) إثل

Description: A fast-growing evergreen tree, up to 3–12 m high. Rounded or irregular spreading crown of many heavy, stout branches and long, drooping twigs. Bark reddish-brown, becoming thick and deeply furrowed into long narrow ridges on the trunk and smooth on the branches. Twigs wiry, very slender, and jointed. Leaves are tiny scales and sheath-like, with a short pointed apex. Flowers pinkish or white.

Importance and uses: Local use for building material and firewood. Widespread cover for wild animals. Recently, bioactive ingredients have been extracted as safe bio-acaricides. Highly valued for stabilizing sand dunes due to its fast growth, with deep, extensive root systems and the ability to resist burial by shifting sand.

Ecology and distribution: Considered a soil accumulator plant. Grows well in saline soil, desert wadis, and sandy plains. Common in the Park's coastal zone, especially in the Wadi El Gemal delta, Sharm al-Luli, and Umm al-'Abas.

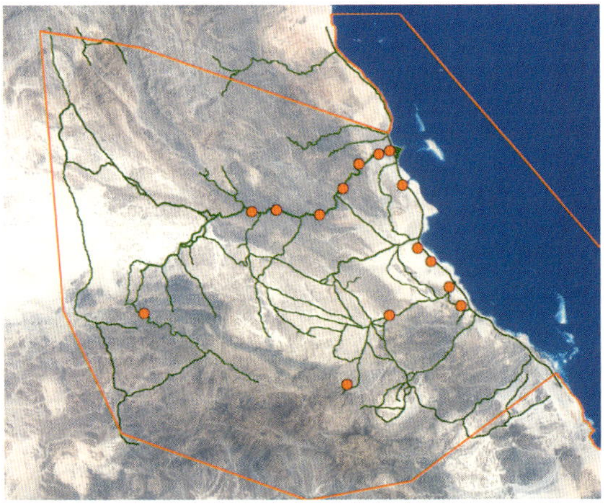

Tamarix nilotica

(Ehrenb.) Bunge, 1852 (Tamaricaceae)

Common English name: Saltcedar

Common local name: (Turfa) طرفة

Description: A multiform species, varying from a shrub to a tree 3–7 m high. Reddish-brown bark, the young parts glabrous. Leaves sessile, slightly clasping, and with deltoid to lanceolate blade. Flowers white to pale pink, in lateral and slender racemes. Has salt-secreting glands through which it is able to expel surplus salt in its leaves and stems.

Importance and uses: Historically, it was the main source of Biblical manna. Local use for secondary timber and for grazing. In other regions used for treatment of hemorrhoids.

Ecology and distribution: Grows in saline sandy soil, at the edges of salt marshes, coastal and inland sandy plains. Distribution controlled by elevation and moisture; hence most are found in wadis, quickly re-establishing after floods. A dominant plant in downstream areas like Wadi El Gemal Delta, Sharm al-Luli, and Umm al-'Abas. Can withstand floods, stabilizing the underlying surface to trap and accumulate sediments.

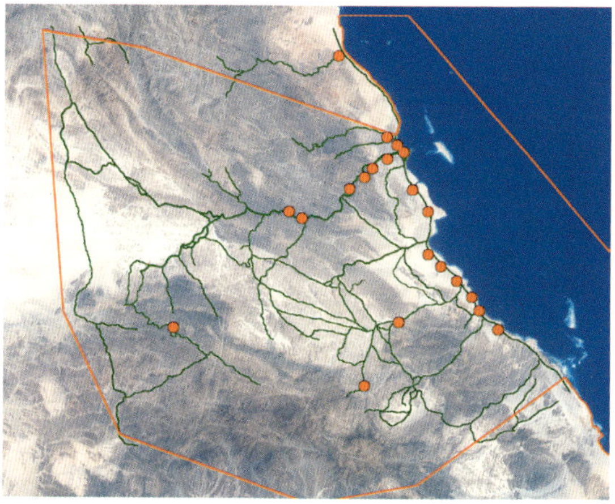

Taverniera aegyptiaca

Boiss., 1849 (Leguminosa)

Common local name: (Dahasir) دهاسير

Description: A perennial shrub up to 40–100 cm high. Stem much-branched. Leaves thick, obcordate, glabrous on the upper surface and white strigose on the lower. Flowers rose-colored, the corolla persistent around the legume until maturity. Legume flattened, spiny, and breaking into two or three segments with one seed. The spiny legumes assist in the dispersing process by attaching themselves to animals.

Importance and uses: Grazing, especially in the dry seasons. No local medicinal value. Recently, six new triterpenoidal saponins have been isolated from this plant.

Ecology and distribution: Grows in stony wadis and sandy plains. Rare all over the Park. Recorded only in Hankurab and the northern boundary in the coastal plain.

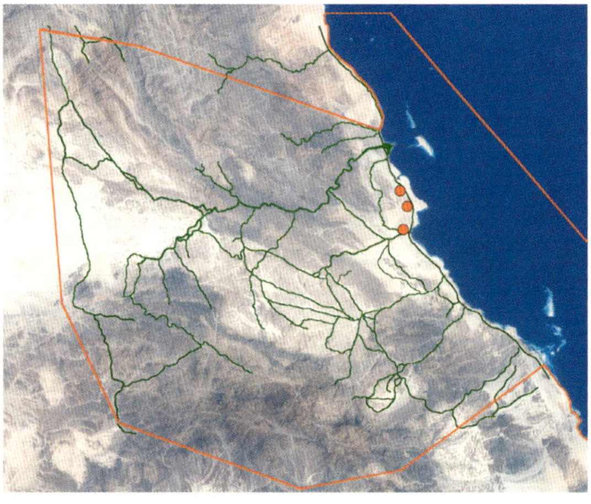

Tephrosia purpurea

(L.) Pers., 1807 (Leguminosa)

Common English name: Purple tephrosia, Wild indigo
Common local name: ('Amayi) عمايى
Description: A deep-rooted, bush-like, short-lived perennial herb, up to 60–90 cm high, remaining green throughout the dry season. Stem erect, imparipinnate leaves with oblong-elliptic leaflets. Leaves, stem, and legumes silvery-strigose. Flowers reddish purple. Legume up to 5.5 cm long, slightly curved upward toward the tip.
Importance and uses: Readily eaten by livestock. Seeds preferred by the sandgrouse. In some other regions the crushed leaves are used as a decoction against snake-bite. Roots, leaves, seeds, and bark are used for the intestines, inflammation, diarrhea, and stimulating appetite.
Ecology and distribution: Prefers sandy soil. Common in Kabb al-Khawwara and Umm al-'Abas.

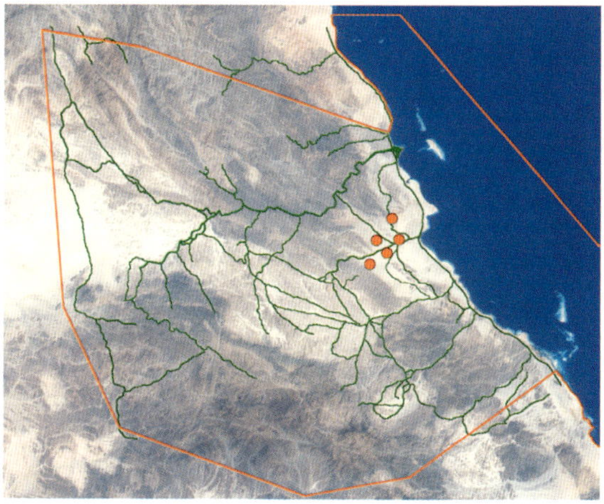

Tribulus megistopterus subsp. *pterocarpus*

(Ehrenb.) Hosni, 1991 (Zygopyllaceae)

Common local name: (Gutub) قطب

Description: A hispid-pilose annual herb. Hairy prostrate branches up to 30–60 cm long. Leaves compound, consisting of five to seven pairs of leaflets. Flowers yellow. The fruit mericarps sparsely covered with short hair and semicircular crenate wings. Mericarps of *T. megistopterus* are bigger than those of *T. Terrestris*.

Importance and uses: Grazing. No other local use.

Ecology and distribution: Grows in sandy plains. Not common in the Park. Recorded in Abu Ghusun and Wadi El Gemal.

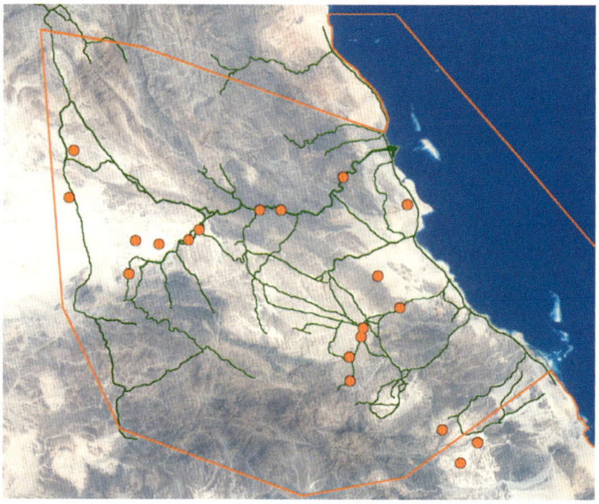

Tribulus terrestris

L., 1753 (Zygopyllaceae)

Common English name: Puncture vine

Common local name: (Gutub) قطب

Description: An annual herb with hairy and prostrate branches up to 90 cm long, spreading from the base. Leaves pinnately compound with linear stipules. Flowers solitary and bright yellow. Seeds contained in mericarps that are densely crested and tuberculate on dorsal side and densely hairy to glabrescent. Mericarps have two long, spreading, and two short downwardly directed spines, painful when trodden on.

Importance and uses: Grazing. *T. Terrestris* considered almost a super herb, with high medicinal value around the world. Extract used as a natural nutritional supplement, and for centuries by the Chinese to calm the liver and treat premature ejaculation. Modern studies demonstrate that it is a natural aid to help impotence, low libido, and male infertility. Enhances energy and vitality.

Ecology and distribution: Grows in sandy soil. Recorded in Wadi El Gemal, al-Khashir, and al-Ri‘da.

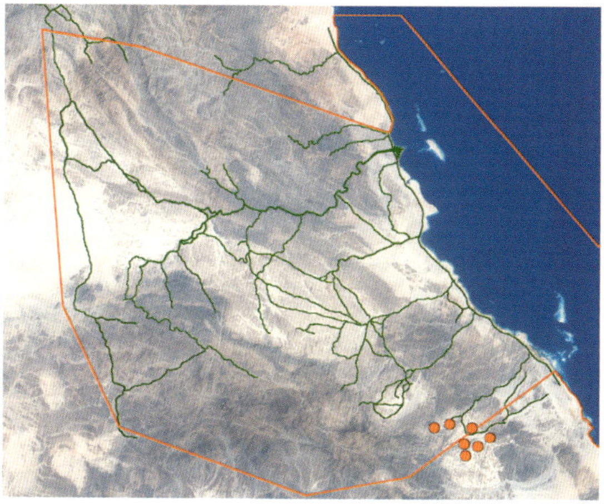

Trichodesma africanum
(L.) Br., 1810 (Boraginaceae)

Trichodesma ehrenbergii
Schweinf., 1869

Common English name: African Trichodesma
Common local name: (Humhum) حمحم
Description: *T. africanum* is an annual or short-lived perennial shrub. Richly branched, usually with woody base, densely covered with rigid, bulbous-based prickles. Leaves opposite, oblong-lanceolate, covered with erect patent prickles on both surfaces. Flowers in clusters, pale blue outside, yellowish-brown inside.

T. ehrenbergii (top, right) resembles *T. africanum* (top, left), but with cordate leaves. Same local name.
Importance and uses: Good pasture for camels. Recently, trichodesmine and pyrrolizidine alkaloids were detected in alkaloid extracts of the aerial parts.
Ecology and distribution Grows in sandy and gravelly wadis. Common in the Park. Recorded in Wadi El Gemal, Durunkat, Hulus, Hafafit, and Abu Ghusun.

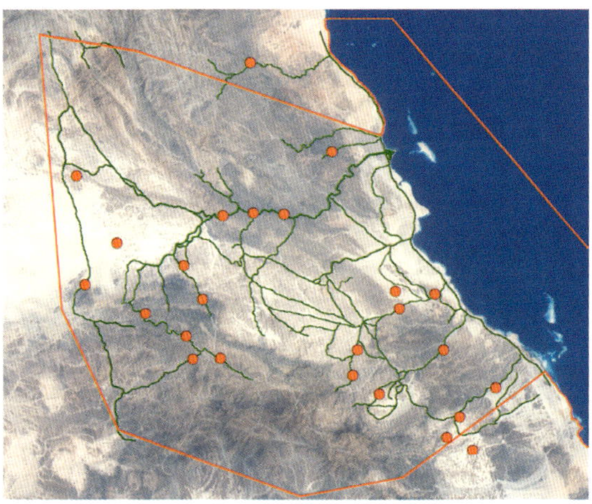

Volutaria lipii

(L.) DC., 1838 (Cmpositae)

Common English name: Volutaria

Common local name: (Khizaran) خيزران

Description: A scabrid annual, up to 70 cm high. Stem branched. Leaves pinnatisect, lobes remotely serrate. Capitula solitary or in clusters. Phyllaries have brown margins and spiny acuminate apex. Corolla purplish-pink.

Importance and uses: Grazing. No other local value.

Ecology and distribution: Grows in desert wadis. Rare in the Park. Recorded in Hangaliya, Wadi El Gemal, and Hulus.

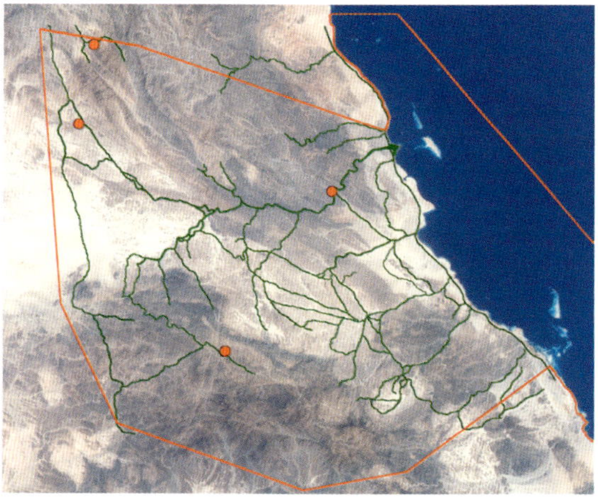

Zilla spinosa

(L.) Prantl, 1891 (Crucifera)

Common English name: Spiny Zilla

Common local name: (Bisilla) بسلة

Description: A perennial shrub up to 1 m high. Grows in dome-like clusters, and can stay green for several years after rain. Branches have many strong spines. Flowers pinkish-purple, sometimes pale mauve. Fruits nutlet-shaped.

Importance and uses: Zilla and Acacia are considered the most important grazing plants. Also important for wild animals like gazelle, wild rabbits, and Nubian ibex. Used as firewood when dry. Used medicinally in other regions to treat urinary tract diseases. Modern studies demonstrate that *Z. spinosa* contains some kinds of saponin and gums.

Ecology and distribution: *Zilla* is a genus specific to the Saharo-Arabian region. The most common plant in the Park. Recorded in all wadis.

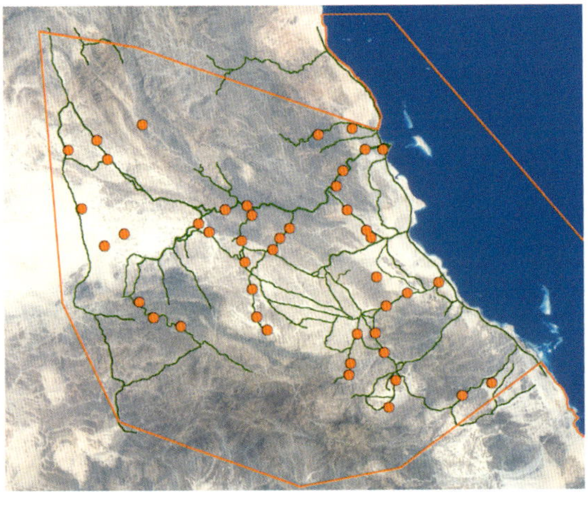

Ziziphus spina-christi

(L.) Desf., 1798 (Rahmnaceae)

Common English name: Christ's thorn, Jujube
Common local name: (Sidr) سدر
Other common names: (Nabag) نبق
Description: A big tree up to 8 meters high, with a huge trunk up to 1 m in diameter. Leaves alternate, oval, finely toothed, and with straight or slightly hooked spiny stipules. Flowers very small, greenish-yellow, and in clusters. Flowers from September to December. Fruits green, changing to yellowish brown at maturity.
Importance and uses:. One of plants mentioned in the Holy Quran. Delicious, edible one-seeded drupe. No local medicinal use. In the Nile Delta and Sinai, considerable medicinal use: a decoction of leaves for colds and hypertension; an infusion of leaves as an astringent anthelminthic, antidiarrhoric, demulcent, depurative, anodyne, pectoral, stomachic, and tonic.
Ecology and distribution: Rare in the Park. Recorded in Hulus only.

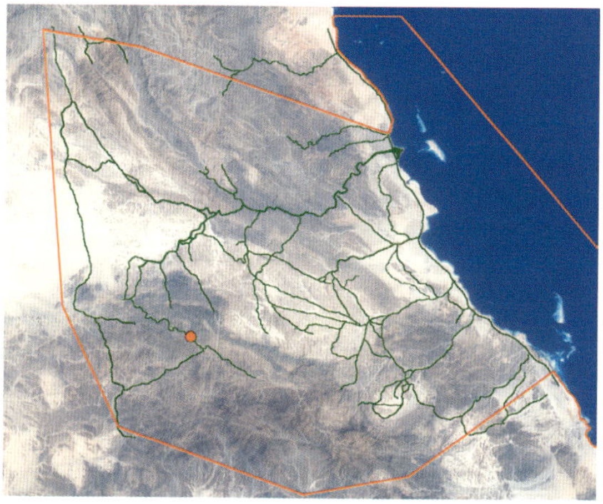

Zygophyllum album

L., 1762 (Zygophyllaceae)

Common local name: (Bihtinay) بحتناى

Description: A mealy-pubescent, low perennial shrub. Succulent, silvery-green to blue-green. Cushion-shaped and often sand-accumulating, building small dunes. Leaves whitish and stipulate. Flowers solitary and white.

Importance and uses: No grazing value. Local use to stimulate appetite. Cairo University researchers recently isolated an antidiarrhoeal compound from the plant.

Ecology and distribution: Usually found in close proximity to the beach. Recorded on the Park's coast, in all islands and also about 2 km into Umm al-'Abas.

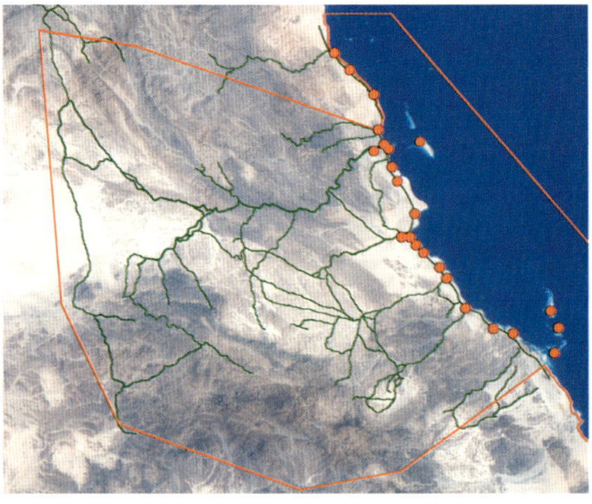

Zygophyllum coccineum

L., 1753 (Zygophyllaceae)

Common local name: (Bawwal) بوال

Description: A succulent undershrub, up to 75 cm high. Two leaflets, over 10 mm long, cylindrical, bright green to yellowish green, fleshy and carried on a long fleshy petiole. Flowers white. Capsule five-valved, about 1 cm long, with obtuse apex. Leaflets and sometimes petioles dropped under severe dry conditions (reducing the transpiring surface).

Importance and uses: Local use to enhance appetite. Modern studies indicate that it may be used as anthelmintic, diuretic, and for flatulent colic. Zygophyllin and Quinovic acid, which exhibit anti-inflammatory activity, have also been isolated from this plant.

Ecology and distribution: Very common in the limestone wadis of the eastern desert. Recorded all over the Park coast and deep into Wadi El Gemal, al-Ghadir, Umm al-'Abas, and Abu Ghusun.

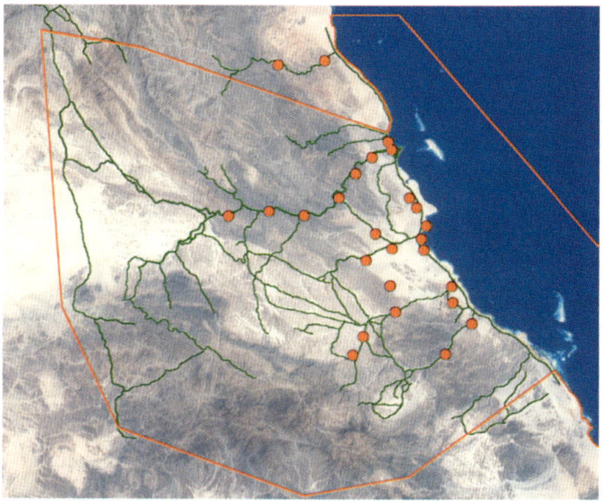

Zygophyllum simplex

L., 1767 (Zygophyllaceae)

Common local name: (Garmal) قرمل

Description: An annual prostrate herb, glabrous, and much-branched. Stem and branches pale-green or purplish, minutely striate. Leaves succulent, simple, sessile, oblong-cylindric, and with stipules. Flowers yellow, fading to white. Seeds oblong, enclosed in five-seeded capsules.

Importance and uses: Grazing. No local medicinal use. In other regions, infusions of leaves and seeds are applied to the eyes in cases of opthalmia and leucoma. Seeds anthelmintic, and used as food by nomads.

Ecology and distribution: Very common in sandy, rocky, and saline habitats. Recorded in all wadis after the rainy season.

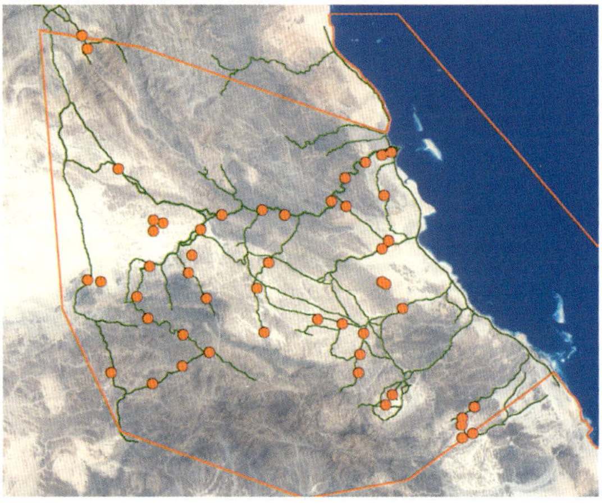

Glossary

achenes (n.): very small, one-seeded fruit, typical of the largest plant family, the sunflower family (Compositae)

apex (n.): tip, pointed end

appressed (adj.): pressed closely to or lying flat against

ascending (adj.): rising after a prostrate portion

auriculate (adj.): ear-shaped; with the leaf base composed of two rounded lobes

bracts (n.): a modified leaf providing an axil for a flower or inflorescence to grow from, or found on a flowering stem

caducous (adj.): falling off soon after formation (not persistent)

calyx (n.): a protective structure around a flower formed by the sepals collectively

capitate (adj.): terminated by an enlarged and rounded head

capitulum (n.): (pl.: capitula) compact cluster of sessile flowers

carpel (n.): collectively the stigma, style, and ovary; the female reproductive parts of a flower

catkin (n.): a spike-like inflorescence of unisexual, apetalous flowers, often pendent and falling as a unit.

cauline (adj.): of or belonging to the stem

clone (n.): a plant produced by asexual reproduction, e.g., from cuttings.

compound leaf (n.): blade divided into leaflets

compressed (adj.): flattened longitudinally

cordate (adj.): heart-shaped; in the form of two rounded lobes

coriaceous (adj.): leathery

corolla (n.): the inner whorl of petals in a flower

corymbose (adj.): clustered flowers

culms (n.): stem of a grass (Gramineae) or a sedge (Cyperaceae)

cuneate (adj.): wedge-shaped

cylindrical (adj.): forming a nearly true cylinder

cyme (n.): flat-topped inflorescence with the oldest flowers at the end of main axis (includes simple, compound, and scorpioid cymes)

cymose (adj.): in the manner of a cyme

deciduous (adj.): with leaves that fall periodically

decurrent (adj.): running down the stem; facing downward

dentate (adj.): toothed; leafedge

depressed (adj.): flattened vertically

digitate (adj.): palmate, with narrower segments

dioecious (adj.): a species population containing male plants bearing only male flowers and female plants bearing only female flowers

distichous (adj.): arranged in two rows on opposite sides of a stem and thus in the same plane

divaricate (adj.): spreading wide

drupes: a fleshy fruit, such as a peach, plum, or cherry, usually having a single hard stone that encloses a seed. Also called stone fruit.

ellipsoidal (adj.): in the form of an ellipse

elliptic (adj.): ellipse-shaped

endemic (adj.): restricted to a certain geographical location

entire (adj.): totally free from division or interruption

epiphytic (adj.): growing on other plants (usually trees) without deriving or contributing nutritional benefit from them

falcate (adj.): sickle-shaped; curved with parallel edges

farinose (adj.): covered with a meal-like powder or minute particles

filiform (adj.): thread-like; in the form of a filament; coarser than capilliform

flavonoids (n.pl.) common plant pigment compounds that act as antioxidants, enhance the effects of vitamin C, and strengthen connective tissue around capillaries

floret (n.): each of the small flowers making up a composite flower-head

foetid (adj.): stinking, offensive, also fetid

follicle (n.): a fruit arising from a single carpel opening along the inner suture

fusiform (adj.): spindle-shaped, tapering at both ends

geniculate (adj.): bent like a knee

glabrescent (adj.): tending to be glabrous

glabrous (adj.): smooth; hairless

glaucous (adj.): covered with a whitish powder or waxy coating as of grapes
globose (adj.): forming a nearly true sphere
glomerate (adj.): clustered compactly
gynodioecious (adj.): of a species with some plants bearing bisexual flowers only, and other plants female flowers
halophyte (n.): plants adapted to saline soils, with seeds that can geminate in saline soil
helicoid (adj.): tending to a helical shape or pattern
hirsute (adj.): hairy
hispid (adj.): covered by rigid hairs
imbricate (adj.): overlapping in a tile-like manner
imparipinnate (adj.): odd number of leaflets, terminated by single leaflet
indigenous (adj.): native
indumentum (n.): the surface hairs of a plant or constituent part, especially where dense
inflated (adj.): bladdery; swollen and transparent, or appearing so
inflorescence (n.): a cluster of flowers, all flowers arising from the main stem axis or peduncle
internode (n.): section of stem between leaves or buds
intricated (adj.) : very complicated; tangled
involucre (n.):: cluster of bracts
labiate (adj.): of corolla or calyx where divided into unequal divisions
lanceolate (adj.) : tapering in shape, like a spear-head; elliptical with a length–breadth ratio of between 3:1 and 6:1
leaflet (n.): a division of the leaf blade in a compound leaf
legume (n.): fruit of Leguminosa; also called a pod
linear (adj.): narrow with untapering margins
mericarps (n.): seed-containing part of a fruit, usually derived from carpel
midrib (n.): the central rib of a leaf
monoecious (adj.): having unisexual male flowers and female flowers on the same plant
mucronate (adj.): terminating in a sharp point, more acute than the leaf from which it projects
nodes (n.): the part of the stem at which leaves, flowers, and branches originate
oblique (adj.): (usually of a leaf) having unequal sides; almost symmetrical
oblong (adj.): broadly elliptical with blunt ends

obovate (adj.): ovate with the narrow end at the base
obovoid (adj.): upside-down ovoid
obtuse (adj.): terminating in a blunt, unpointed end; forming an angle of more than 90 degrees
ovate (adj.): egg-shaped; oval, with one end more pointed than the other
ovoid (adj.): egg-shaped; ovate
palmate (adj.): five-lobed, with the midribs joined at a common point
panicle (n.): a branched or compound raceme (i.e., main rachis with branches bearing flowers on pedicels).
papillose (adj.): bearing minute, pimple like protuberances
paripinnate (adj.): evenly pinnate, terminated by two opposite leaflets
pedicel (n.): any small, stalk-like structure
peduncle (n.): the stalk of a flower, inflorescence, or fruit
perianth (n.): the collective parts of the calyx and corolla when these are similar; the outer part of a flower
pericarp (n.): the part of a fruit formed from the wall of a ripened ovary
petal (n.): the floral modified leaves of a flower that comprise the corolla
petiolate (adj.): relating to, or in the form of a petiole
phyllaries (n.): in Compositae, bracts surrounding the capitulum, often referred to as bracts of involucre
pilose (adj.): hairy, with rather long, patent simple hairs
pinnae (n.): leaflets of a pinnate leaf
pinnate (adj.): divided into central axis and lateral ribs or leaflets, like a feather
pinnatifid (adj.): pinnately lobed, with shallow lobes
pinnatipartite (adj.): pinnately divided to about halfway
pinnatisect (adj.): pinnately divided almost to the midrib
pinnules (n.): the leaflets of a bipinnate leaf, a second order pinna
pruinose (adj.): frosted with white powder
puberulous (adj.): somewhat pubescent
pubescent (adj.): with a hairy surface
pungent (adj.): tapering evenly to a sharp point
pyrrolizidine alkaloids: Alkaloids found in various species as *Senecio* spp. and *Crotalaria* spp. There are at least ten different chemicals, many of them hepatotoxic, teratogenic, and carcinogenic.
raceme (n.): unbranched inflorescence with flowers on pedicels
rachis (n.): axis to which leaflets are attached in compound leaves

reniform (adj.): kidney-shaped; an oval with the ends curved around in the same direction
rhomboid (adj.): diamond-shaped
rosette (n.): a circular growth pattern with leaves growing radially from a central point; rose-shaped
scabrid (adj.): rough to touch, usually from the presence of minute stiff hairs
scarious (adj.): having a dry membranous appearance
sessile (adj.): attached directly; stalkless; immobile
siliqua (n.): fruit of Crucifera plants, like *Farsetia* sp.
simple leaf (n.): has one blade
sinuate (adj.): lyrate, but with the lobes more equally sized
sori (n.): groups or clusters of sporangia (spores containers), of pteridophytes
spatulate (adj.): spoon-shaped
spike (n.): unbranched inflorescence with sessile flowers (no pedicels)
spur (n.): usually slender hollow projection formed by the fused bases of the lower petals in some flowers, often containing nectar
stellate (adj.): star-shaped
stipule (n.): a small modified leaf usually found at the base of a leaf
subulate (adj.): awl-shaped, like a stout needle, linear-lanceolate
tendril (n.): a slender leafless shoot produced by many Nepenthes and other climbing plants as an aid to climbing
tepal (n.): any of the modified leaves making up a perianth
terete (adj.): smooth and rounded; circular, or nearly so, in section but not necessarily cylindrical
terminal (adj.): borne at the end of a stem.
ternate (adj.): arranged in a whorl or cluster of three
tomentose (adj.): covered in tomentum
tomentum (n.): matted woolly threads on the surface of leaves and stems
truncate (adj.): (of leaves, etc.) cut off at the end; an abrubt termination as if the tip has been cut cleanly off
tubular (adj.): forming a hollow nearly true cylinder
turgid (adj.): swollen
umbel (n.): flat-topped inflorescence with all the pedicels arising from a common point (includes simple and compound umbels)
undulate (adj.): wavy; alternately concave and convex
vermiculate (adj.): worm-shaped

vermifuge (adj.): anthelminthic, cure fom worms
verticil (n.): a circular arrangement of parts around an axis; a whorl
viscid (adj.): covered with sticky or resinous secretion

List of Plants by Abbadi Name

Latin name	Local (Abbadi) name	الاسم المحلى (العبادى)	page
Salvia aegyptiaca	*Ibsiwi*	إبْسِوى	120
Tamarix aphylla	*Itl*	إتل	128
Aerva javanica	*Ara*	أرا	33
Salvadora persica	*Arak*	أراك	119
Cotula cinerea	*Aribyan*	اربيان	64
Calligonum polygonoides subsp. *Comosum*	*Arta*	أرطى	47
Arnebia hispidissima	*Atan*	أتان	37
Zygophyllum album	*Bihtinay*	بحتناى	138
Asphodelus tenuifolius	*Barwag*	بَرْوَق	40
Zilla spinosa	*Bisilla*	بسلة	136
Lavandula coronopifolia	*Baswi*	بَسْوى	88
Iphiona scabra	*Bakanun*	بكانون	85
Zygophyllum coccineum	*Bawwal*	بوال	139
Phragmites australis	*Bus*	بوص	108
Astragalus vogelii subsp. *fatmensis*	*Tawil*	تاويل	42
Astragalus vogelii subsp. *vogelii*	*Tawil*	تاويل	42
Morettia philaeana	*Taghar*	تغر	98

Latin name	Local (Abbadi) name	الاسم المحلى (العبادى)	page
Ficus palmata	*Tin barri*	تين برى	77
Pulicaria undulata subsp. *undulata*	*Jitya*	جيتيا	113
Cuscuta sp.	*Hamul*	حامول	68
Aizoon canariense	*Hidak*	حداك	34
Solenostemma arghel	*Hargal*	حرجل	126
Imperata cylindrica	*Halfa*	حلفا	83
Rumex vesicarius	*Hummad*	حماض	117
Commicarpus helenae	*Hummad al-jabal*	حماض الجبل	61
Trichodesma africanum	*Humhum*	حمحم	134
Trichodesma ehrenbergii	*Humhum*	حمحم	134
Citrullus colocynthis	*Handal*	حنضل	54
Cucumis prophetarum	*Hinidlan*	حنضلان	67
Malva parviflora	*Khubbayza*	خبيزة	97
Salsola imbricata	*Khrayt*	خريط	118
Reseda pruinosa	*Khuzama*	خزامة	115
Blepharis edulis	*Khashir*	خشير	46
Volutaria lipii	*Khizaran*	خيزران	135
Rhus tripartita	*Dablut*	دبلوت	116
Cometes abyssinica	*Dagn al-shaykh*	دقن الشيخ	60
Caylusea hexagyna	*Danaban*	دنبان	51
Aeluropus lagopoides	*Dahasir*	دهاسير	32
Taverniera aegyptiaca	*Dahasir*	دهاسير	130
Hyphaene thebaica	*Dom*	دوم	82
Pulicaria incisa	*Rabul, Shay al-jabal*	ربل، شاى الجبل	112
Heliotropium bacciferum	*Rumram*	رمرام	80
Echinops spinosissimus	*Siha, Singid*	سِحا ، سِنقِد	70

Latin name	Local (Abbadi) name	الاسم المحلى (العبادى)	page
Ziziphus spina-christi	*Sidr*	سدر	137
Maerua crassifolia	*Sarh*	سرح	96
Neurada procumbens	*Sa'dan*	سعدان	100
Acacia ehrenbergiana	*Salam*	سلم	27
Juncus rigidus	*Samar*	سمار	86
Acacia tortilis subsp. tortilis	*Samur*	سمر	30
Senna alexandrina	*Sana abbali*	سنا ابالى	123
Senna italica	*Sanamikki*	سنامكى	124
Lycium shawii	*Sahanun*	سهانون	95
Suaeda monoica	*Suwwayda*	سويدة	127
Plantago exigua	*Swigat*	سويقات	111
Acacia tortilis subsp. raddiana	*Sayyal*	سيال	29
Convolvulus hystrix	*Shibrig*	شبرق	62
Indigofera spinosa	*Shadid*	شديد	84
Limonium axillare	*Shalil*	شليل	90
Arthrocnemum macrostachyum	*Shunan*	شنان	39
Sarcocornia fruiticosa	*Shunan*	شنان	121
Panicum turgidum	*Shush*	شوش	104
Cornulaca monacantha	*Shuk al-dib, Had*	شوك الديب ، حاد	63
Artemisia judaica	*Shih*	شيح	38
Cleome chrysantha	*Sifiraya*	صفراية	57
Cleome brachycarpa	*Sifirayat al-dan*	صفراية الضان	56
Tamarix nilotica	*Turfa*	طرفة	129
Capparis decidua	*Tundub*	طندب	49
Cleome amblyocarpa	*'Abal al-'ajuz, 'Uffayn 'atmud*	عبل العجوز، عفين عتمود	55
Glossonema boveanum	*'Itr*	عتر	79

Latin name	Local (Abbadi) name	الاسم المحلى (العبادى)	page
Acacia etbaica	*'Arad*	عرض	28
Calotropis procera	*'Ushar*	عشار	48
Lotononis platycarpa	*'Ishib*	عِشِبْ	92
Cyperus conglomeratus	*'Ishub*	عشوب	69
Cleome dorserifolia	*'Uffayn*	عفين	58
Cocculus pendulus	*'Ullig*	عليق	59
Tephrosia purpurea	*'Amayi*	عمايى	131
Lindenbergia indica	*'Ud al-zughut*	عود الزغط	91
Nitraria retusa	*Ghargad*	غرقد	101
Pergularia tomentosa	*Ghalga*	غلقة	105
Astragalus eremophilus	*Faga'ay*	فجعاى	41
Ochradenus baccatus	*Gurdi*	قرضى	102
Zygophyllum simplex	*Garmal*	قرمل	140
Lotus hebranicus	*Gadub*	قضب	94
Lotus glinoides	*Gudayb*	قضيب	93
Tribulus megistopterus subsp. *pterocarpus*	*Gutub*	قطب	132
Tribulus terrestris	*Gutub*	قطب	133
Crotalaria microphylla	*Giliglan*	قليقلان	66
Hippocrepis constricta	*Giliglan*	قليقلان	81
Echium horridum	*Kahali*	كحالى	71
Erodium laciniatum	*Kiryayit*	كريايت	72
Adiantum capillus-veneris	*Kusbarat al-bir*	كزبرة البئر	31
Fagonia mollis	*Kasha'id al-hamir*	كشائيد الحمير	74
Anastatica hierochuntica	*Kaff Maryam,* *Umm Kammash*	كف مريم ، أمّ كَمّاشْ	36
Euphorbia granulata	*Lubbayn*	لبين	73

Latin name	Local (Abbadi) name	الاسم المحلى (العبادى)	page
Amaranthus graecizans	*Lisan al-tayr*	لسان الطير	35
Chenopodium murale	*Lisan al-tayr*	لسان الطير	52
Forsskaolea tenacissima	*Lussaq*	لصاق	78
Capparis spinosa	*Lasaf*	لصف	50
Moringa peregrina	*Maya*	مايا	99
Leptadenia pyrotechnica	*Markh*	مرخ	89
Periploca angustifolia	*Murrikh*	مريخ	106
Silene linearis	*Miswig*	مِسويقْ	125
Avicennia marina	*Shura, Manjaruf*	شورى ، منجروف	44
Crotalaria aegyptiaca	*Natash*	نتش	65
Phoenix dactylifera	*Nakhl*	نخل	107
Chrozophora tinctoria	*Nila*	نيلة	53
Balanites aegyptiaca	*Higlig, Balah al-sukkar, Lalub*	هجليج ، بلح السكر، لالوب	45
Senecio flavus	*Hadhadid*	هدهديد	122
Orobanche cernua	*Haluk*	هلوك	103
Abutilon fruticosum	*Hambuk*	همبوك	26
Atriplex farinosa	*Handa'al, Hawa*	هندآل، حوا	43
Farsetia longisiliqua	*Huk*	هوك	75
Farsetia stylosa	*Huk 'atmud*	هوك عتمود	76
Plantago ciliata	*Hulagayt*	هولاقيت	110
Plantago amplexicaulis	*Hulagayt*	هولاقيت	109
Reichardia tingitana	*Hiwwi' al-kilab*	هويع الكلاب	114
Kickxia acerbiana	*Widin al-far*	ودين الفار	87

Plant Families and Species Identified in WGNP

FAMILY	No. of species	Plant species
ACANTHACEAE	**1**	*Blepharis edulis*
ADIANTACEAE	**1**	*Adiantum capillus-veneris*
AIZONACEAE	**1**	*Aizoon canariense*
AMARANTHACEAE	**2**	*Aerva javanica* *Amaranthus graecizans*
ANACARDEACEA	**1**	*Rhus tripartita*
ASCLEPIADACEAE	**6**	*Calotropis procera* *Glossonema boveanum* *Leptadenia pyrotechnica* *Pergularia tomentosa* *Periploca angustifolia* *Solenostemma arghel*
AVICENIACEAE	**1**	*Avicennia marina*
BALANITACEAE	**1**	*Balanites aegyptiaca*
BERBERIDACEAE	**1**	*Cocculus pendulus*
BORAGINACEAE	**5**	*Arnebia hispidissima* *Echium horridum* *Heliotropium bacciferum* *Trichodesma ehrenbergii* *Trichodesma africanum*

FAMILY	No. of species	Plant species
CAPPARACEAE	**7**	*Capparis decidua* *Capparis spinosa* *Cleome amblyocarpa* *Cleome brachycarpa* *Cleome chrysantha* *Cleome dorserifolia* *Maerua crassifolia*
CARYOPHYLLACEAE	**2**	*Cometes abyssinica* *Silene linearis*
CHENOPODIACEAE	**7**	*Arthrocnemum macrostachyum* *Atriplex farinosa* *Chenopodium murale* *Cornulaca monacantha* *Salsola imbricata* *Sarcocornia fruiticosa* *Suaeda monoica*
COMPOSITAE	**9**	*Artemisia judaica* *Cotula cinerea* *Echinops spinosissimus* *Iphiona scabra* *Pulicaria incisa* *Pulicaria undulata* subsp. *undulata* *Reichardia tingitana* *Senecio flavus* *Volutaria lipii*
CONVOLVULACEAE	**2**	*Convolvulus hystrix* *Cuscuta* sp.
CRUCIFERA	**7**	*Anastatica hierochuntica* *Farsetia longisiliqua* *Farsetia stylosa* *Morettia philaeana* *Zilla spinosa* *Citrullus colocynthis* *Cucumis prophetarum*
CYPERACEAE	**1**	*Cyperus conglomerates*

FAMILY	No. of species	Plant species
EUPHORBIACEA		*Chrozophora tinctoria* *Euphorbia granulata*
GERANIACEAE	**1**	*Erodium laciniatum*
GRAMINEAE	**4**	*Aeluropus lagopoides* *Imperata cylindrica* *Panicum turgidum* *Phragmites australis*
JUNCACEAE	**1**	*Juncus rigidus*
LABIATAE	**2**	*Lavandula coronopifolia* *Salvia aegyptiaca*
LEGUMINOSAE	**18**	*Acacia ehrenbergiana* *Acacia etbaica* *Acacia tortilis* subsp. *raddiana* *Acacia tortilis* subsp. *tortilis* *Astragalus eremophilus* *Astragalus vogelii* subsp. *fatmensis* *Astragalus vogelii* subsp. *vogelii* *Crotalaria aegyptiaca* *Crotalaria microphylla* *Hippocrepis constricta* *Indigofera spinosa* *Lotononis platycarpa* *Lotus glinoides* *Lotus hebranicus* *Senna alexandrina* *Senna italica* *Taverniera aegyptiaca* *Tephrosia purpurea* subsp. *apollinea*
LILIACEA	**1**	*Asphodelus tenuifolius*
MALVACEAE	**2**	*Abutilon fruticosum* *Malva parviflora*
MORACEAE	**1**	*Ficus palmata*
MORINGACEAE	**1**	*Moringa peregrina*

FAMILY	No. of species	Plant species
NITRARIACEAE	**1**	*Nitraria retusa*
NIYCTAGINACEAE	**1**	*Commicarpus helenae*
NURADACEAE	**1**	*Neurada procumbens*
OROBANCHACEAE	**1**	*Orobanche cernua*
PALMAE	**2**	*Hyphaene thebaica* *Phoenix dactylifera*
PLANTAGINACEAE	**3**	*Plantago amplexicaulis* *Plantago ciliata* *Plantago exigua*
PLUMBAGINACEAE	**1**	*Limonium axillare*
POLYGONACEAE	**2**	*Calligonum polygonoides* subsp. *comosum* *Rumex vesicarius*
RAHMNACEAE	**1**	*Ziziphus spina-christi*
RESEDACEAE	**3**	*Caylusea hexagyna* *Ochradenus baccatus* *Reseda pruinosa*
SALVADORACEAE	**1**	*Salvadora persica*
SCROPHULARIACEAE	**2**	*Kickxia acerbiana* *Lindenbergia indica*
SOLANACEAE	**1**	*Lycium shawii*
TAMARICACEAE	**2**	*Tamarix aphylla* *Tamarix nilotica*
URTICACEAE	**1**	*Forsskaolea tenacissima*
ZYGOPHYLLACEAE	**6**	*Fagonia mollis* *Tribulus megistopterus* subsp. *pterocarpus* *Tribulus terrestris* *Zygophyllum album* *Zygophyllum coccineum* *Zygophyllum simplex*

References

Abd El-Ghani, M.M. 1998. Environmental correlates of species distribution in arid desert ecosystems of eastern Egypt. *Journal of Arid Environments* 38:97–313.

———. 2000. Vegetation composition of Egyptian inland saltmarshes. *Botanical Bulletin of Academia Sinica* 41:305–14.

Abd El-Ghani, M.M., and K.N. Abde-Khalik. 2006. Floristic diversity and phytogeography of the Jabal Elba National Park, South-east Egypt. *Turkish Journal of Botany* 30:121–36.

Abd El Rahman, H., and L. Krzywinski, 2008. Environmental effects on morphology of Acacia tortilis group in the Red Sea Hills, North-eastern Sudan and South-eastern Egypt. *Forest Ecology and Management* 255:254–63.

Ahmad, H., G.R. Bhatti, and A. Latif. 2004. Medicinal flora of the Thar Desert: an overview of problems and their feasible solutions. *Zonas Áridas* 8.

Al-Mufti, M. 2000. Flora of Nabq protected area. Cairo: Egyptian Environmental Affairs Agency.

Ali, M.M., G. Dickinson, and K.J. Murphy. 2000. Predictors of plant diversity in a hyperarid desert wadi ecosystem. *Journal of Arid Environments* 45:215–30.

Allaby, M. 2002. *Basics of Environmental Science*. 2nd edn. London: Routledge.

Allam, A.R., E. Saaf, and M.A. Dawoud. 2003. Desalination of brackish groundwater in Egypt. *Desalination* 152(1–3): 19–26.

Altimimi, M.A.K. 2002. Organization and characterization of floral structures in indigenous Thimam (Panicum turgidum), under UAE Environment. *Journal of Agricultural Research* 4:1–11.

Badri, A.M., and A.I. Hamed. 2000. Nutrient value of plants in an extremely arid Nutrient value of plants in an extremely arid environment (Wadi Allaqi Biosphere Reserve, Egypt). *Journal of Arid Environments* 44:347–56.

Bahaa-Eddin, S. 2003. Management plan for Wadi el-Gemal-Hamata Protected Area. Internal report for the Egyptian Environmental Affairs Agency.

Barakat, H.N., 2003. Evaluation of the flora and plant communities in Wadi El Gemal-Hamata protected area. Internal report for EEAA/PSU.

Barnes, J. 2004. *Herbal medicines*. 2nd edn. London: Pharmaceutical Press.

Baslar, S., and H.H. Mert. 1999. Studies on the ecology of *Chrozophora tinctoria L.* and *Rubia tinctorum L.* in Western Anatolia. *Turkish Journal of Botany* 23 (1999): 33–44.

Batanouny, K.H. 1999. *Wild medicinal plants in Egypt*. Cairo: The Palm Press.

Belal, A.E., B. Leith, J. Solway, and I. Springuel. 1998. Environmental valuation and management of plants in Wadi Allaqi, Egypt. International Development Research Center (IDRC) Canada.

Boulos, L. 1983. *Medicinal Plants of North Africa*. Michigan: Reference Publications, Inc.

———. 1999. *Flora of Egypt*, vol. 1. Cairo: al-Hadara Publishing.

———. 2000. *Flora of Egypt*, vol. 2. Cairo: al-Hadara Publishing.

———. 2002. *Flora of Egypt*, vol. 3. Cairo: al-Hadara Publishing.

———. 2005. *Flora of Egypt*, vol. 4. Cairo: al-Hadara Publishing.

———. 2009. *Flora of Egypt Checklist*, Cairo: Al-Hadara Publishing.

Brandes, D. 2005.*Calotropis procera on Fuerteventura* <http://www.biblio.tubs.de/geobot/calotropis.pdf>.

Briggsa, J., M. Badri, and A. Mekki. 1999. Indigenous knowledges and vegetation use among Bedouin in the Eastern Desert of Egypt. *Applied Geography* 19:87–103.

Brown, G. et al. 2003. *Coastal and terrestrial ecosystem management requirements in the GCC states*. Abu Dhabi: Erwda.

Cabello, J., D. Alcaraz, and F. Gómez-Mercado. 2003. Habitat, occurrence and conservation of Saharo-Arabian-Turanian element Forsskaolea tenacissima L. in the Iberian Peninsula. *Journal of Arid Environments* 53:491–500.

Chapagain, B., and Z. Wiesman. 2005. Larvicidal effects of aqueous extracts of Balanites aegyptiaca (desert date) against the larvae of Culex pipiens mosquitoes. *African Journal of Biotechnology* 4/11:1351–54.

De Paiva, Selma Ribeiro, Shirely da Silva Marques, Maria Raquel Figueiredo, Maria Auxiladora Coelho Kaplan. 2003. Plumbaginales: A pharmacological approach. Plumbaginales: A pharmacological approach. Floresta e Ambiente 10/1:98–105.

El-Demerdash, M.A., A.K. Hegazy, and A.M. Zilay. 1995. Vegetation-soil relationships in Tihamah coastal plains of Jazan region, Saudi Arabia. *Journal of Arid Environments* 30:161–74.

Dodd, R.S., F. Blasco, Z.A. Rafii, and E. Torquebiau. 1999. Mangroves of the United Arab Emirates: ecotypic diversity in cuticular waxes at the bioclimatic extreme. *Aquatic Botany* 63:291–304.

Ferreira, T.O. 2007. Are mangrove forest substrates sediments or soils? A case study in southeastern Brazil. *Catena* 70:79–91.

Forti, M. et al. 2006. Long-term plant survival and development under dryland conditions in an experimental site in the semi-arid Negev of Israel. *Journal of Arid Environments* 65:1–28.

Frantzen, J. 2000. Disease epidemics and plant competition: control of Senecio vulgaris with Puccinia lagenophorae. *Basic and Applied Ecol*olgy 1:141–48.

Gallacher, D.J., and J.P. Hill. 2006. Effects of camel grazing on the ecology of small perennial plants in the Dubai (UAE) inland desert. *Journal of Arid Environments* 66:738–50.

Ghazanfar, S.A. 2004. Biology of the central desert of Oman. *Turkish Journal of Botany* 28:65–71.

Guenther, R. 2005. Vegetation and grazing in the St. Katherine Protectorate, south Sinai, Egypt. Report on plant surveys done during Operation Wallacea expeditions.

Haggag, M.Y. 2002. *Herbal medicine in Egypt.* Centre International de Hautes Etudes Agronomiques Mediterraneennes (CIHEAM) Options Mediterranéennes (45–55).

Harraz, F.H., and A. Ulubelen, 1995. Dammarane triterpenes from Cleome Ambl yocarpa. *Phytochemistry* 39 (1): 17–178.

Hashem, F.A., and H.E. Wahba. 2000. Isothiocyanates in myrosinase treated herb extract of Cleome chrysantha Decne. and their antimicrobial activities. *Phytotherapy Research Journal* 14 (4): 284–87.

Hegazi, A.M. et al. 2005. Egyptian National Action Program to Combat Desertification. Desert Research Center.

Hegazi, A.M., and I.H. el-Bagouri. 2002. National action plan for combating desertification.

Hegazy, A.K., O. Hammouda, J. Lovett-Doust, and N.H. Gomaa. 2008. Population dynamics of Moringa peregrina along altitudinal gradient in the northwestern sector of the Red Sea. *Journal of Arid Environments* 72:1537–51.

Heneidak, S., R.J. Grayer, and G.C. Kite. 2006. Flavonoid glycosides from Egyptian species of the tribe Asclepiadeae (Apocynaceae, subfamily sclepiadoideae). *Biochemical Systematics and Ecology* 34:575–84.

Henkel, A. 1911. American Medicinal Leaves and Herbs. Washington, D.C.: Government Printing Office.

Kassas M. 1999. Rescuing drylands: a project for the world. *Futures* 31:949–58.

———. 1995. Desertification: a general review. *Journal of Arid Environments* 30: 115–28.

———. 1957. On the ecology of the Red Sea coastal land. *Journal of Ecology* 45:187–203.

———. 1953. Habitat and plant communities in the Egyptian desert. II: the features of a desert community. *Journal of Ecology* 40 (2): 248–56.

———. 1952. Habitat and plant communities in the Egyptian desert. *Journal of Ecology* 40 (2): 342–51.

Kassas, M., and W.A. Girgis. 1964. Habitat and plant communities in the Egyptian desert. V: the limestone plateau *.Journal of Ecology* 52 (1): 107–19.

Kassas, M., and M. Imam. 1959. Habitat and plant communities in the Egyptian desert. IV: the gravel desert. *Journal of Ecology* 47 (2): 289–310.

———. 1954. Habitat and plant communities in the Egyptian desert. III The wadi bed ecosystem. *Journal of Ecology* 42 (2): 24–441.

Khalil, R., and D. Aly. 2003. *Egypt's Natural Heritage*. 2nd edn. Singapore: SNP Sprint Pt.

Khare, C.P. 2007. Indian medicinal plants. Berlin/Heidelberg: Springer-Verlag.

Larsen, H.O., and C.S. Olsen. 2007. Unsustainable collection and unfair trade? Uncovering and assessing assumptions regarding Central Himalayan medicinal plant conservation. *Biodivers Conserv* 16:1679–97.

Lioubimtseva, E.U. 1995. Landscape changes in the Saharo-Arabian area during the last glacial cycle. *Journal of Arid Environments* 30:1–17.

Mahmoud, Tamer. 2009. "Medicinal Plants of Wadi El Gemal National Park." Internal report for Nature Conservation Sector, Egyptian Environmental Affairs Agency, Cairo.

Moor, M. 1995. *An Herbal/Medical Dictionary*. Albuquerque, New Mexico.

Mossallam, H.A. and A.A. BaZaid. 2000. *An illustrated guide to the wild plants of Taif. Kingdom of Saudi Arabia*. Saudi Arabia: Publication Committee For Tourism Activation-Taif.

Mostafa, A.A., R.H. Abd El-Wahab, Mohammed Saad Zahgloul, Tamer Mahmoud. 2007. Status of medical plants as a soure of income and job creation for local community residents in WGHPA and related areas. Egypt Life Red Sea Project, Task Order No.: 263-M-00-04-00032-00.

Moustafa, A.A., and M.S. Zaghloul. 1996. Environment and vegetation in the mountain Saint Catherine area, south Sinai, Egypt. *Journal of Arid Environments* 34: 331–49.

El-Naggar, E.M.B. et al. 2005. Antidiabetic effect of cleome droserifolia aerial parts: lipid peroxidation–induced oxidative stress in diabetic rats. *Acta Veterinaria Brno* 74: 347–52.

Noy-Meir, I. 1974. Desert ecosystems: higher trophic levels. *Annual Review of Ecology and Systematic* 5:195–214.

O'Leary, J.W., and E.P. Glenn. 1994. Global distribution and potential for halophytes, in V.R. Squires and A. Ayoub, eds., *Halophytes as a resource for livestock and rehabilitation of degraded lands*, pp. 7–17. Netherlands: Kluwer Academic.

Razek, M.S., M. Dorgham, M. Atta, M. Beltagi, and K. Kamel. 1998a. Mission to establish a model of conservation and management of mangroove ecosystems. Part 1. The Northern Sector (Hurghada–Qusseir). For the GEF Project.

———. 1998b. Mission to Establish a Model of Conservation and Management of Mangrove Ecosystems. Part 2. The Southern Sector (Abu Ghusun–Hamata). For the GEF Project.

Ross, I. 2005. Medicinal plants of the world, vol. 3, pp. 623. Totowa, NJ: Humana Press Totowa.

Saleh, M.A. 2007. Assessment of mangrove vegetation on Abu Minqar Island of the Red Sea. *Journal of Arid Environments* 68:331–36.

Shaltout, K.H., M.G. Sheded, and Y.M. Al-Sodany. 2003. Phytosociology and size structure of Nitraria retusa along the Egyptian Red Sea coast. *Journal of Arid Environments* 53:331–45.

Shivkar, Y.M., and V.L. Kumar. 2003. Histamine mediates the proinflammatory effect of latex of Calotropis procera in rats. *Mediators of Inflammation* 12 (5): 299/302.

Springuel, I. 2006. *The Desert Garden*. Cairo: The American University in Cairo Press.

Springuel, I., and A. Mekki. 2002. Value of Desert Plants. Razek, M.S., M. Dorgham, M. Atta, M. Beltagi, and K. Kamel. I. Acacia Trees in Wadi Allaqi Conservation Area. Allaqi Project Working Paper No. 20.

Täckholm, V. 1974. *Students' Flora of Egypt*. 2nd edn. Beirut: Cairo University Press.

El-Tahir, M.M., I.B. el-Tayeb, and S.A. Shaddad. 2005. The pharmacological actions of the aqueous extract of the leaves of Solenostemma argel (Hayne) on isolated rabbit aortic strip and guinea pig atria. *Journal of Animal and Veterinary Advances* 4 (10): 831–34.

Al-Turki, T.A. 2004. A prelude to the study of the flora of Jabal Fayfa in Saudi Arabia. *Kuwait Journal of Science and Engineering* 31(2): 77–145.

Woldewahid, G. et al. 2007.Description of plant communities on the Red Sea coastal plain of Sudan. *Journal of Arid Environments* 68:113–31.

Zahran, M.A, and A.J. Willis. 2009. *The Vegetation of Egypt*, 2nd edn. Netherlands: Springer.